PRACTICING GRAMMAR AND USAGE

Muriel Harris

with revisions by
David Davis

PRENTICE HALL
REFERENCE GUIDE
TO GRAMMAR AND USAGE

FIFTH EDITION

Muriel Harris

Johnson County Community College

Prentice Hall, Upper Saddle River, New Jersey 07458

©2003 by PEARSON EDUCATION, INC.
Upper Saddle River, New Jersey 07458

ISBN 0-13-098220-2

Printed in the United States of America

CONTENTS

PART ONE

THE WRITING PROCESS

Chapter 1

Purposes and Audiences

1a. Purpose

For each of the purposes for writing listed below, create a situation in which you might write with that purpose in mind. An example of a situation for the first purpose, "Summarizing," is given here.

EXAMPLE

Summarizing:

> I work for a consumer finance company, and my job is to look over an applicant's credit history: credit report, information from the application, etc. I must summarize the credit history in a single paragraph for the loan officer who will make the final decision.

1. Summarizing:

   _____

   _____

   _____

   _____

2. Defining:

   _____

   _____

   _____

   _____

3. Analyzing:

_____

_____

_____

_____

4. Persuading:

_____

_____

_____

_____

5. Reporting:

_____

_____

_____

_____

6. Evaluating:

_____

_____

_____

_____

7. Discussing/Examining:

_____

_____

_____

_____

8. Interpreting:

_____

_____

_____

_____

1b. Topic

In order to find a topic for a piece of writing, assume that an interviewer or reporter is asking you the following questions, and write your responses to those questions. An example of a possible answer to the first question is given here.

EXAMPLE

What is a problem you'd like to solve?

Businesses downtown have a problem attracting customers since there is nowhere to park; a parking garage might help revitalize the city.

1. What is a problem you'd like to solve?

_____

_____

_____

_____

2. What is something that pleases, puzzles, irritates, or bothers you?

_____

_____

_____

_____

3. What is something you'd like to convince others of?

_____

_____

_____

_____

4. What is something that seems to contradict what you read or see around you?

_____

_____

_____

_____

5. What is something you'd like to learn more about?

_____

_____

_____

_____

6. What is something you know about that others around you may not know?

_____

_____

_____

_____

1c. Thesis

Narrow each of the following topics by asking yourself the series of questions listed with each topic. Then write the thesis that has developed from your answers. Analyze your thesis by underlining your topic once and your comment about it twice. An example is given here.

EXAMPLE

Topic: Carpentry

Who am I in this piece of writing? I am someone with knowledge to share.

Who is my intended audience? Readers of a do-it-yourself newsletter.

What is the purpose of this writing? To inform.

What are some other conditions that will shape this writing? Length (space provided in the newsletter for this article), format, demographics of the audience (age, basic level of knowledge of carpentry).

Thesis: <u>Building an attractive and efficient computer desk</u> can be an easy and affordable weekend project.

1. Topic: Television

    Who am I in this piece of writing? _____

    Who is my intended audience? _____

    What is the purpose of this writing? _____

    What are some other conditions that will shape this writing? _____

    _____

    Thesis: _____

    _____

    _____

    _____

2. Topic: Human cloning

    Who am I in this piece of writing? _____

    Who is my intended audience? _____

    What is the purpose of this writing? _____

    What are some other conditions that will shape this writing? _____

    _____

    Thesis: _____

    _____

    _____

    _____

3. Topic: Sports

    Who am I in this piece of writing? _____

    Who is my intended audience? _____

    What is the purpose of this writing? _____

What are some other conditions that will shape this writing? _____

_____

Thesis: _____

_____

_____

_____

Chapter 2

Writing Processes and Strategies

2a. Planning

Use the planning strategies listed below to find material you might want to include in writing about the corresponding topics. An example of one planning strategy, "Brainstorming," is given here.

EXAMPLE

Topic: Choosing a college

Planning Strategy: Brainstorming

deciding between a state university and a private college
    reasons to go to a state university
        • close to home
        • in-state tuition much less than private college
        • large selection of classes
        • popular sports teams
        • research facilities

    reasons to go to a private college
        • smaller classes
        • prestige
        • less chance of being lost in the crowd
        • even freshmen always taught by professors

checking out college flyers
checking out magazine articles on colleges
visiting college campuses
talking to friends and family who have attended college
knowing how much I can afford and not going above it
grades/acceptance
what SAT/ACT scores are required
choosing a roommate

1. Topic: Paying for college

    Planning Strategy: Brainstorming

    _____

    _____

_____

_____

_____

2. Topic: Comparing American dating to dating in another culture

   Planning Strategy: Freewriting

   _____

   _____

   _____

   _____

3. Topic: Rock music

   Planning Strategy: Listing

   _____

   _____

   _____

   _____

4. Topic: Violence on television

   Planning Strategy: Clustering and Branching

   _____

   _____

   _____

   _____

5. Topic: How to choose a college

   Planning Strategy: Outlining

   _____

   _____

   _____

   _____

   _____

6. Topic: Drinking and driving

   Planning Strategy: Who?—what?—when?—where?—how?—why?

   _____

   _____

   _____

   _____

   _____

2b–2c. Drafting and Organizing

Using one of the topics and planning strategies you completed in 2a, draft and organize a paper on that topic.

   _____

   _____

   _____

   _____

   _____

   _____

   _____

   _____

_____

_____

_____

_____

_____

_____

_____

_____

_____

2d. Collaborating

Using one of the following methods, get responses from readers of the draft of the paper you completed in 2b–2c: meeting with a writing-center tutor, meeting with a small group of students in your class, or meeting with a writing group you form on your own. Ask your readers to respond to the questions below about your paper, and record their responses to each question.

1. What do the readers like about this draft?

   _____

   _____

2. What do the readers think is the main point of this paper?

   _____

   _____

3. Are there any sections that are unclear and need more explanation?

   _____

   _____

4. Does the paper fit the assignment?

   _____

   _____

5. Who is the appropriate reader or audience for the paper?

_____

_____

6. Are there any sections of the paper that seem out of order?

_____

_____

7. Are there any sections of the paper where the writing seems to digress from the topic?

_____

_____

8. Does the paper flow?

_____

_____

9. What else do your readers want to know about the paper's topic?

_____

_____

10. What is the most important revision to your paper your readers would suggest?

_____

_____

2e. Revising

Using the responses you gathered in 2d and the revision checklist of higher-order concerns (HOCs), revise your paper for greater effectiveness.

_____

_____

_____

_____

_____

_____

_____

_____

_____

_____

_____

_____

_____

_____

_____

2f. Editing and Proofreading

Using the checklist of later-order concerns (LOCs), edit your paper for details of grammar, usage, punctuation, spelling, and other mechanics. After editing for LOCs, proofread your paper one last time for missing words, misspellings, and format. Then write the final draft of your paper below.

_____

_____

_____

_____

_____

_____

_____

_____

Chapter 3

Paragraphs

3a. Unity

Read the sample paragraph below, and then write a short paragraph describing what aspects of unity are present or missing.

      A recent expedition to Tibet resulted in the discovery of a previously unknown species of a small horse. The horses are only about four feet tall, but they are very strong. Expedition members experienced a great deal of bad weather during their stay in Tibet. Even though the discovery of the tiny horses caused much excitement in the scientific world, the local citizens seem to take them for granted and use them as pack animals.

_____

_____

_____

_____

_____

_____

_____

_____

3b. Coherence

Read the sample paragraph below, and then write a short paragraph describing what aspects of coherence are present or missing.

      Although many people think of the interior of Alaska as flat expanses of ice and snow, the geography of the area is actually quite varied. The interior of Alaska has long, cold winters and mild, short summers. The climate is actually quite dry, but most of the precipitation that does fall is in the winter and is in the form of snow. Twenty-three languages are spoken in the interior of Alaska. The area was home to forest dwelling bands of natives in historic times.

_____

_____

_____

_____

_____

_____

_____

_____

3c. Development

Read the sample paragraph below, and then write a short paragraph describing whether its development is adequate or inadequate and why.

> *Blade II* is a really good movie. It stars Wesley Snipes and is about vampires. It is really exciting and is a sequel to the first movie – Blade.

_____

_____

_____

_____

_____

_____

_____

_____

_____

3d. Introductions and Conclusions

Ask several classmates how they go about writing an introductory paragraph for a longer piece of writing. Write a short paragraph describing the different ways people draft an introductory paragraph.

_____

_____

_____

_____

_____

_____

_____

_____

_____

_____

Ask several classmates how they go about writing a concluding paragraph for a longer piece of writing. Write a short paragraph describing the different ways people draft a conclusion.

_____

_____

_____

_____

_____

_____

_____

_____

_____

3e. Patterns of Organization

For each of the patterns of organization listed below, write a paragraph using that pattern on the topic provided.

1. Pattern of Organization: Narration

   Topic: An experience that taught you a valuable lesson

   _____

   _____

   _____

   _____

   _____

   _____

   _____

   _____

   _____

2. Pattern of Organization: Description

   Topic: A place where you go to think

   _____

   _____

   _____

   _____

   _____

   _____

   _____

   _____

   _____

3. Pattern of Organization: Cause and Effect

   Topic: Why you chose your current major/course schedule

   _____

   _____

   _____

   _____

   _____

   _____

   _____

   _____

   _____

   _____

4. Pattern of Organization: Analogy

   Topic: The impact of the Internet on American society

   _____

   _____

   _____

   _____

   _____

   _____

   _____

   _____

   _____

5. Pattern of Organization: Example

   Topic: Contemporary heroes

   _____

   _____

   _____

   _____

   _____

   _____

   _____

   _____

6. Pattern of Organization: Illustration

   Topic: "Reality" television shows

   _____

   _____

   _____

   _____

   _____

   _____

   _____

   _____

7. Pattern of Organization: Classification

   Topic: Contemporary music

   _____

   _____

   _____

   _____

   _____

   _____

   _____

   _____

   _____

   _____

8. Pattern of Organization: Division

   Topic: College life

   _____

   _____

   _____

   _____

   _____

   _____

   _____

   _____

   _____

   _____

9. Pattern of Organization: Process Analysis

   Topic: Finding a job

   _____

   _____

   _____

   _____

   _____

   _____

   _____

   _____

   _____

10. Pattern of Organization: Compare and Contrast

   Topic: Two places you have visited

   _____

   _____

   _____

   _____

   _____

   _____

   _____

   _____

   _____

   _____

11. Pattern of Organization: Definition

Topic: Success

_____

_____

_____

_____

_____

_____

_____

_____

_____

_____

Chapter 4

Argument

4a–4c. Writing and Reading Arguments, Considering the Audience, and Finding a Topic

Choose a topic for a persuasive paper which is arguable, interesting, or of local concern. Once you have chosen your topic, decide on the appropriate audience for your topic, your purpose for the argument, the kinds of appeals you will use to make your case, and the common ground you share with your audience. If you have difficulty coming up with a topic of your own, you may choose from one of the following: smoking laws; the role of the United States as a world peacekeeper; the use of personality tests as a requirement for employment; a particular investment method as opposed to others (for example, investing in mutual funds as opposed to the stock market); or a local bond issue.

Topic _____

Audience _____

Purpose_____

Appeals_____

_____

Common Ground _____

_____

4d. Developing Your Arguments

Using the same topic for writing and the ideas you began planning in the last exercise, begin developing your argument by clarifying what your main point or claim is, what support you will offer for that claim, what warrants or unspoken assumptions are present in the argument, and what form of development (inductive or deductive) will be most effective.

Your claim _____

The type of support you will use to convince the audience _____

_____

Warrants in the argument _____

_____

Method of development (inductive or deductive) _____

Consider how to avoid errors in reasoning in your argument by writing examples of logical fallacies about your topic which you would NOT use in a persuasive paper. By recognizing what you will not use as an argument, you will be better prepared to decide what you will use.

1. Hasty Generalization _____

    _____

2. Begging the Question (circular reasoning)_____

    _____

3. Doubtful Cause (post hoc, ergo propter hoc) _____

    _____

4. Using Irrelevant Proof to Support a Claim (non-sequitur)_____

    _____

5. False Analogy _____

    _____

6. Attack the Person (ad hominem) _____

    _____

7. Either . . . Or_____

    _____

8. Bandwagon_____

    _____

4e. Organizing Your Arguments

Decide upon the most effective organization for your argument and justify why you have chosen that pattern of organization.

Pattern of Organization _____

Justification _____

_____

(Now that you have completed Exercises 4a–4e, you should be prepared to draft, revise, and edit a persuasive paper on your topic if your instructor requires it.)

Chapter 5

Writing with Computers

5a. Planning with Computers

Freewrite or brainstorm using the computer to find a topic for writing and to gather ideas for your topic. You may want to turn down the brightness on your computer so that the screen is dark and you can't see what you're typing. Allow your mind to jump from idea to idea, and don't worry about grammar or mechanics. Write for about five minutes. Then go back to what you have written and use the underline function to underline ideas that you think may be useable for a piece of writing. Next, use the cut and paste feature of your computer to place the ideas you have underlined into a draft. Then use the space below to write a brief paragraph about your reaction to using the computer to freewrite or brainstorm. You may want to discuss whether you felt comfortable with the strategy and whether you found it useful or not and why.

Using the same topic for writing and the ideas you began planning in the last exercise, use the computer to set up headings for an outline in large, bold letters. After you set up the headings, go back and fill in subheadings and subpoints to create the larger structure of the paper. Then use the space below to write a brief paragraph about your reaction to using the computer to outline.

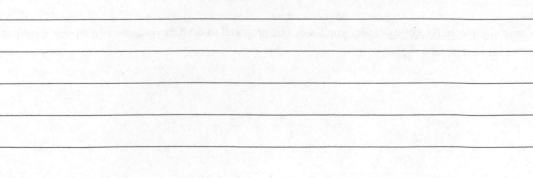

_____

_____

_____

_____

5b. Drafting with Computers

Using the outline you created in the last exercise, begin drafting your piece of writing using the computer. You may want to split the screen or open two windows so that your outline file is open at the same time you are working on your draft file. That way you can refer to your outline as you write your draft. As you write your draft, write reminders to yourself in bold letters or in parentheses about ideas to improve your paper later or questions that you need to check later. Don't worry at this point about your draft looking messy or about manuscript issues such as line spacing or margins. After you have finished your first draft, use the space below to write a brief paragraph about your reaction to using the computer to draft.

_____

_____

_____

_____

_____

_____

_____

_____

_____

5c. Organizing with Computers

Using the draft you created in the last exercise, make a new copy of your file. Then, in the new file, use the cut and paste feature of the computer to move paragraphs around to see if there may be a better method of organizing your writing than the one you used to begin with. Choose the best method of organization and save it as your draft, using a file name that lets you know it is the most recent version. Use the space below to write a brief paragraph about your reaction to using the computer to organize.

_____

_____

_____

_____

_____

_____

_____

_____

5d. Revising with Computers

Using the draft you saved in the last exercise, go to the beginning of your document and examine it for development and organization. You may want to hit the return key after every sentence so that every sentence looks like a separate paragraph. Then check to see if all of your sentences are about the same length. If they are, you probably need to work on sentence variety. Also check to see if all of your sentences start the same way. If they do, you probably need to work on using a variety of sentence patterns. Make the necessary revisions, and then use the space below to write a brief paragraph about your reaction to using the computer to revise. You can also highlight words or sentences and drag them to new locations to change the delivery style and add variety.

_____

_____

_____

_____

_____

_____

_____

_____

5e. Editing and Proofreading with Computers

Using the revised draft you completed in the last exercise, use the computer to edit and proofread your writing. Check your draft for spelling, grammar, and mechanics. You may want to use your computer's spell checker, grammar checker, and thesaurus as you edit. Try putting active verbs in bold print and passive constructions in italics, and try using larger fonts for descriptive words. By doing so, you may find that some of your writing habits need to be changed, such as using too many passives or too few descriptive words. Then use the space below to write a brief paragraph about your reaction to using the computer to edit and proofread.

_____

_____

_____

_____

_____

_____

_____

_____

_____

_____

(Now that you have completed 5a–5e and made all the changes necessary to your draft, you should have a completed piece of writing and should be ready to print your final draft to turn in if your instructor requires it.)

PART TWO

SENTENCE ACCURACY, CLARITY, AND VARIETY

Chapter 6

Comma Splices and Fused Sentences

The following paragraph contains some sentences that are punctuated incorrectly, some comma splices, and some fused sentences. Correct all the punctuation errors.

Our country seems to be going through a change in attitudes. Unlike our forefathers, we Americans are now encouraged to get as much as possible as quickly as possible. This attitude is expressed on television advertising also plays on this appeal. Many see a relationship between these current attitudes and gambling on lotteries, it is easy to understand why more and more people are handing their money over to chance, fate and luck if what they are looking for is instant gratification. Statistics show this attitude is growing, in the late 80s, state lotteries grew an average of 17.5 percent annually—roughly as fast as the computer industry. High-tech advertising for the lotteries takes attention away from the fact that a player has virtually no chance of winning, advertisements focus instead on the fantasy of what it would be like to win. Surveys conducted by state lotteries show that few players have a clear understanding of how dismal their odds of winning really are, a player has a better chance of being struck by lightening than of winning a lottery.

Chapter 7

Subject-Verb Agreement

In the following paragraph, underline the verb that agrees with the subject.

A business that is growing rapidly in popularity as well as in profits (is, are) selling meteorites to collectors, museums, universities, and research laboratories. The usual meteorite that dealers offer to customers (weigh, weighs) only a few grams or less, but sometimes, someone out collecting meteorites (find, finds) a piece that can weigh over 100 pounds. Either a whole large meteorite or some chunks (sells, sell) for thousands of dollars. But in some countries the government (is, are) beginning to pass laws that forbid the export of meteorites. None of these governments (want, wants) these national treasures to leave their countries. The price for meteorites (depend, depends) on the rarity of that kind. How much is known to exist (is, are) an important factor in determining the rarity of any specimen that is found. Of the three classes of meteorites, "irons"—made up of iron and nickel—are common, though they represent less than 10 percent of all meteorites that (strike, strikes) the Earth. But they survive the intense heat of entering the atmosphere better than other meteorites (does, do) and can be easily found with a metal detector. All other meteorites, which (is, are) made of stone, are the most common ones that are found. Among these there (is, are) some that may have come from nearby planets when meteorites hit their surfaces. Having a piece of Mars (is, are) a good way to start a collection.

As you complete the following sentences, make sure the verb agrees with the subject. For this exercise, use only present or past tense verbs. For example, you could write I am happy, or I was happy, but do not write I will be happy.

1. I _____

_____

2. We _____

_____

3. Nearly all of my sister's clothes which she wears to school _____

_____

4. The store clerks and their manager _____

_____

5. Either Carlos or his brothers _____

_____

6. Not only the players but also the coach _____

_____

7. What I want to explain _____

_____

8. To feel successful _____

_____

9. Each _____

_____

10. Some of the examples _____

_____

11. Some of the assignment _____

_____

12. The committee _____

_____

13. Cryogenics _____

_____

14. The scissors _____

_____

15. Acme Enterprises _____

_____

16. Her idea (complete this sentence using a linking verb) _____

_____

17. Magazine articles (complete this sentence using a linking verb) _____

_____

18. There _____ an interesting book on the history of television in the library.

19. There _____ many books on the history of television in the library.

20. It _____ his beliefs that formed the basis for his argument.

21. They are the people who _____

_____

22. She is the person who _____

_____

23. Mr. Baker is one of those instructors who _____

_____

Chapter 8

Sentence Fragments

The following paragraph has both fragments and complete sentences. Identify each sentence as either a fragment or a complete sentence.

(1) A fierce battle has developed in American schools over the question of using English in the classroom. (2) Historically, immigrants coming to America were expected to learn English and to be taught in English. (3) Though that did not mean that they had to reject their original culture of language. (4) But for many, using English in school meant that their ethnic legacy would no longer dominate. (5) That it would disappear as they became fluent English speakers. (6) As a result, the emphasis on English as the dominant language was seen by many as discriminatory. (7) While others see this emphasis as the only way to have a common American culture that all children can share. (8) One answer to this has been bilingual education in which children who speak another language are taught academic subjects in their native language. (9) This transitional program which helps them to move along through school while they acquire English. (10) Bilingual education being the answer for some who want to preserve children's culture and provide schooling for them as they learn English. (11) Although others see it as a failed system because it segregates limited-English children into separate classrooms and dooms them to unskilled jobs where competence in English is less important. (12) They point out that children need to learn English in order to get better jobs, go on to college, and become full members of American society.

1. _____
2. _____
3. _____
4. _____
5. _____
6. _____
7. _____
8. _____
9. _____
10. _____

11. _____

12. _____

Chapter 9

Dangling and Misplaced Modifiers

9a. Dangling Modifiers

Underline the dangling modifiers in the following paragraph.

     The great memorials in the nation's capital are slowly deteriorating. Having faced the elements for seven decades, even casual tourists can see that the Lincoln Memorial is wearing down. Water is causing the steel structures embedded in the concrete slabs to deteriorate. At the Jefferson Memorial, which is built on clay fill, the steps are starting to pull away from the base of the monument, and there are cracks appearing in the dome. Being washed daily, details in the marble carvings of both monuments are falling off. Air pollution and acid rain are also contributing to the gradual disintegration. To find a solution, constant studies by the National Park Service are being conducted, but the caretakers of the monuments are pessimistic. Exposure to the elements, they say, causes some deterioration that cannot be stopped. Looking more like ruins than buildings, it is hard to watch these noble monuments wear away.

9b. Misplaced Modifiers

In the following paragraph, underline the misplaced modifiers and rewrite the sentences so that the modifiers are placed more appropriately.

     The Food and Drug Administration (FDA) claims that it has found tiny amounts of drug residue in milk samples in a report issued recently. The level of contamination is so low that there is no real safety problem in the nation's milk supply, but a ban has been put on one drug, sulfamethazine, found in a few samples, to prohibit its use with beef cattle and pigs by farmers. The FDA has already banned the use of sulfamethazine with milk cows. However, there is still concern that some dairy farmers or veterinarians use the drug improperly among members of Congress, even though recent testing of milk samples only found a few traces of sulfa drugs in a large number. The FDA is now calling on dairy farmers and veterinarians to eliminate all illegal uses of veterinary drug products. Farmers are already almost all complying with this order.

9c. Additional Modifier Exercises

Identify each sentence as a misplaced or dangling modifier and rewrite correcting the problem

1. Using primitive tools, scientists have discovered Cro-Magnon man was human.

   _____

2. Bob stunned the pit bull with a large flashlight.

   _____

3. Walking into the house's entryway, the lamp glowed warmly.

   _____

4. Please choose a magazine on the enclosed card.

   _____

5. Sue found an emerald woman's bracelet.

   _____

6. Approaching the city from the west, the sports arena is quite a sight.

   _____

Chapter 10

Parallel Construction

In the following paragraph underline all parallel constructions and rewrite any nonparallel forms so that they are constructed in parallel form.

Recently, two pilots, one in a 175-seat commercial airliner and with the other one in a small, twin-engine corporate jet, were barreling toward each other. On the instrument panel of the commercial jet, a small air traffic screen flashed a yellow circle and a voice announced, "Traffic." As the yellow circle approached the center of the screen, it changed to a red square. The voice said loudly, "Climb, climb." Noticing the red square and as he pulled up, the pilot saw the other craft fly past several hundred feet below. The voice that called out the warning was not the copilot but the latest audiovisual aid to arrive in cockpits of planes, a traffic alert and collision avoidance system. The Federal Aviation Administration has issued an order that this system must be installed in 20 percent of all large commercial planes by next year and to install it in the rest of the large commercial planes using American airspace within the next three years. The system works by computing the distance between planes, warning planes when they get within six miles of each other, and then to decide which plane should climb and which should descend to avoid a collision.

Write a paragraph with at least five sentences in which there are parallel constructions in at least four of the sentences. You may want to write about air safety or airport safety.

_____

_____

_____

_____

_____

_____

_____

_____

Chapter 11

Consistency/Avoiding Shifts

The following paragraph has a number of inconsistent shifts in person and number, in verb tenses, in tone, in voice, and in discourse. Rewrite the paragraph so that it avoids any inconsistent shifting.

High school proms used to be dances where students dressed up in suits and dresses and celebrated their coming graduation, but now you have to spend big bucks for a tuxedo or elegant formal dress. Proms have become big business as formalwear shops and limousine services offer their services in advertising campaigns. Tuxedo rental shops across the country report that proms, not weddings, account for the major proportion of its business. One local shop owner said that he used to look forward to spring as his busy season because of weddings, but now I make more money in the spring because of high school proms. The typical expenses now include the tuxedo rental, prom tickets, corsage, dinner, and limousine rental. You can easily spend $300 on the dance, and that was just for the basics. Prom-goers can spend additional funds for the latest fashions in tuxes, and photos can be bought for $50 or more. Even when the prom is over, there were other expenses. Some kids go away for the whole weekend, often to a resort hotel. So you have to throw in the costs for a hotel, and if parents are along as chaperones, it is necessary to add in the cost of their rooms and meals too. High school graduates insist that this is all necessary as a rite of passage, but the expense is not appreciated by parents who often have to cough up at least part of the funds.

Write a paragraph with at least five sentences in which you pay special attention to consistency in pronoun person and number, verb tense, tone, and voice. You may want to write about high school proms.

_____

_____

_____

_____

_____

_____

_____

Chapter 12

Faulty Predication

The following paragraph has some sentences with faulty predication. Rewrite these sentences so that they are correct.

    With the present concern for the environment, some companies are trying to increase their sales by advertising their products as environmentally safe. The makers of some plastic trash bags, for example, are claiming that their plastic is degradable. The reason for the claim is because there are additives that cause the product to break down after prolonged exposure to sunlight. Biodegradability, they assert, is when there is photodegradability, a breakdown by sunlight. But since most trash bags are buried in landfills, the benefits of photodegradability are questionable. Thus, the government has stated that one way to improve deceptive advertising claims is when they eliminate false or misleading information.

Finish the sentences for each of the subjects listed here. Pay special attention to avoiding faulty predication.

1. The reason is

2. Horror is

3. His excuse was

4. Her proposal was

Chapter 13

Coordination and Subordination

The sentences in the following paragraph can be improved by adding more coordination and subordination. Rewrite the paragraph so that there is more coordination and subordination, but avoid excessive or inappropriate forms of adding clauses together.

Americans have become videotape addicts. Over 75 percent of all American households now have videocassette recorders, so hotels hope to make their guests feel at home by providing equipment for watching videotapes. Some of the largest hotel chains in the country have added videocassette recorders in the rooms which can be used by renting videocassettes from shops in the hotel where there is a good selection of recent movies for guests to view in their rooms. In these hotels guests can show their room key and can rent a movie at a reasonable rate. Other hotels don't want to bother with stores in the lobby, and they are exploring a different option, so they are adding automated video dispensing machines in their lobbies that hold hundreds of titles and have new releases as well as standard favorites. One hotel chain has a lot of large business conventions, and it has investigated another approach. It is offering to distribute to guests videotapes that the corporation holding the convention wants its participants to see since corporations like this because the videotapes can convey some of the key ideas being presented at the convention. Videotape players in hotel rooms may soon be standard equipment, just as television sets were added years ago when Americans became addicted to televisions so that they expected to watch televisions in their hotel rooms.

Chapter 14

Sentence Clarity

The following paragraph has some sentences with clarity problems. Revise the paragraph to improve sentence clarity.

To jot handwritten notes onto an electronic pad may be a new approach to using computers. A special pen that projects a narrow light beam onto the pad is the way this is done. For computer users who have had to rely on entering data into a computer by means of a keyboard, it is a major step forward in using computers. Not having to type is less distracting to many people who are not skilled typists but whose computer usage is high. It has been the goal of computer developers to rid the computer of keyboards for the last twenty-five years. But there has been insufficient development in the field of character recognition as this is necessary for the elimination of keyboards. Teaching computers to read through optical character recognition is one way to eliminate the keyboard. Recognition of the human voice is another way for computers to cease to rely on keyboard inputting of data. Speech recognition is not advancing as rapidly as some computer developers would like, and it is not likely that the near future will see computers we can converse with. We hardly have not appropriate technology that is this advanced. More promising is the ability of the computer to scan images. Already character recognition machines are being used in offices where pages of printed material are scanned by machines. Also under consideration by computer developers are electronic gloves that could be used by people to point to areas of the screen. There is hardly no limit to what will be coming next in computer development. The doing away of the keyboard will result in saving time and in the elimination of all those typos.

Write a paragraph with at least five sentences in which you draw arrows from old information in sentences to new information. Use positive instead of negative, avoid double negatives, and pay special attention to using verbs instead of nouns. Underline any passive voice verbs and be sure that they are appropriate. You may want to write about your experience in using computers.

_____

_____

_____

_____

_____

Chapter 15

Transitions

Rewrite the following paragraph by using transitions to build bridges between the sentences and parts of sentences. Use underlines to indicate the transitions added in your revised version.

My father really needs help. He is a workaholic. He works nearly twelve hours a day. Doctors have told him it is not only bad for his health, but it is affecting his family. He has worried my family to no end. My family has tried to help him. He has not acknowledged the problem. He has a tolerance that goes through the roof. He sneaks out of the house before anyone is awake. He gets home after most of us have finished dinner and are getting ready for bed. He works at home. His computer is connected to the one at his office. His work calls him at home. He has a pager and a cell phone. Things may be getting worse. Dad accepted a promotion to regional director.

Write a paragraph of at least five sentences in which you use transitions in at least four of the sentences. Underline your transitions. You may want to write about your experience with delays in grocery store checkout lines.

_____

_____

_____

_____

_____

_____

_____

_____

_____

Chapter 16

Sentence Variety

The following paragraph has very little sentence variety. Revise the paragraph by using a combination of strategies to add variety.

   Animal rights activists are known primarily for their campaigns against fur coats and the use of animals in laboratories. They are also campaigning against rodeos. Protesters say that rodeo animals are being mistreated. They say the animals are starving and live a life filled with pain and suffering. Animal rights activists also say that rodeo horses buck because they are in pain. Rodeo and circus owners say that this is not so. These animals are well fed and comfortable. These animals would be going to slaughter if they were not used as show animals. Handlers explain that they have a healthy respect for the size and power of these animals. The animals are treated like star athletes. They enjoy performing. Animal rights activists point to the use of cattle prods and bucking straps to get the animals moving. Rodeo owners argue that even ranchers have to use electric prods to get herds moving. Ranchers used pitchforks before prods were used. Calf roping is also condemned by animal rights activists. Roping breaks calves' necks and can also snap vertebrae and legs. Calf roping has been banned in some states. Eliminating calf roping can result in the overall elimination of rodeo shows. Rodeo owners protest that breaking of calves' necks, bones, and vertebrae just doesn't happen. Rodeo owners invite activists to come to rodeos and see for themselves.

Find a paragraph you have written previously that you think needs more sentence variety. Rewrite the paragraph here so that you have combined sentences; added words, phrases, or clauses at the beginning of the sentence; or changed some sentences to dependent clauses within the sentence.

_____

_____

_____

_____

_____

_____

_____

_____

_____

PART THREE

PARTS OF SENTENCES

Chapter 17

Verbs

17a. Verb Phrases

Underline the verb phrases in the following paragraph.

Some scientists are saying that a buildup of carbon dioxide and other greenhouse gases in the atmosphere will cause global warming. But another group of scientists argues that we should study the data more carefully before any firm conclusions are drawn. While scientists generally agree that an unchecked accumulation of greenhouse gases will cause changes, no one knows when it will start, how much will happen, or how rapidly it will occur. The most widely accepted estimate is that there will be a rise in the earth's average temperature as early as 2050. This could bring rising sea levels and severe droughts in some areas. But no one knows yet how clouds and the ocean's ability to absorb heat will affect this. When scientists understand this better, projections can be revised.

Write a paragraph with at least five sentences, and underline the verb phrases. You may want to write more about the greenhouse effect and global warming.

_____

_____

_____

_____

_____

_____

_____

_____

_____

_____

17b. Verb Forms

In the following paragraph, underline verb forms that are part of a verb phrase with one line and verb forms that are used alone with two lines.

The evidence that global warming has started is not very strong. Some scientists believe that the concentration of carbon dioxide has increased over 25 percent since the early 1800s, but other scientists point to the fact that the average global temperature has risen by no more than a half degree Centigrade. Even that rise is questionable since there was a cooling period from 1940 to 1970 that caused forecasters to predict a return to the ice ages. Therefore, to act on predictions by passing laws that restrict or ban the use of fossil fuels may be hasty, but conserving energy, banning harmful chlorofluorocarbons, and planting more trees to absorb carbon dioxide from the air seems sensible. Many industries are also acting more responsibly and are reducing hazardous emissions from their factories.

Write a sentence using each of the following verb forms not as a part of the verb phrase but elsewhere in the sentence.

1. -ing verb

_____

_____

2. -ed verb

_____

_____

3. to + verb

_____

_____

17c. Verb Tense

Underline the correct verb tenses from the choices given in the following paragraph.

In 1987, the FBI (opened, has opened, was opening) a $1.5 million mock-up of a small town in Virginia named Hogan's Alley. Presently, the town's population (has been, will be, is) about 200. Generally, Hogan's Alley (has looked, looks, is looking) like any peaceful little American town, but often the quiet (will be shattered, is shattered, had been shattered) by the sound of a shotgun or squealing tires. Then prospective G-men who (had been sitting, sat, will sit) outside the post office jump in their cars and race after the "criminals." None of this (will be, is, is being) real because Hogan's Alley (is, has been, had been) a training academy for those who (will want, want, will have wanted) to become FBI agents. Next year over 500 trainees (will have attended, attend, will attend) classes in frisking, lectures on handcuffing, and seminars on interrogating witnesses. The FBI (started, was starting, had started) Hogan's Alley because it wanted its agents to have more true-to-life experience before they go out and deal with dangerous criminals. So now every day there (will be, have been, are) mock bank robberies, kidnappings, and drug busts. The "criminals," however, are actors, part-time students, retirees, off-duty policemen and firemen, and anyone else who (has passed, will pass, had passed) the rigorous screening tests.

The following paragraph is written in present tense. At the beginning of the paragraph, add the words "Last year" and rewrite the rest of the paragraph so that it is in past tense. Be especially careful when changing irregular verbs.

In Hogan's Alley, the FBI's mock-up village for prospective FBI agents, the trainees take part in an intensive 14-week training course. About 46 agents move through the program which begins with lessons in surveillance. Trainees track a suspect from his home as he drives to a shopping mall and sells a small bag of phony cocaine. Next comes a class in simple arrests, when agents-in-training burst into a fleabag motel and take an unarmed burglar as he lies in bed. Agents learn how to frisk suspects, and then they read them their rights. Instructors, who bring their own experience as former FBI agents to the teaching, carefully give advice to each trainee and provide pointers on how to handle details such as slipping on handcuffs during a struggle. Nine weeks into the course, trainees get some practice in arresting an armed felon. Their final lessons take place in a courtroom, where they face a team of actors who pose as a tough team of defense lawyers. Those trainees who do not flunk out of the course become FBI agents, and the actors, who play drug peddlers, burglars, and other felons, say that seeing what it is like being on the wrong end of the law reminds them that they do not want to become criminals themselves.

17d. Verb Voice

The following paragraph contains both active and passive voice verb phrases. Indicate the voice by underlining "active" or "passive" in the parentheses.

Like many cities built on a river, Kansas City is divided (active, passive) between two states. The biggest single municipality is Kansas City, Missouri, but over one-half of the population of the metropolitan area lives (active, passive) in various suburban cities on the Kansas side. Problems are created (active, passive) when it comes time to finance projects that will benefit (active, passive) both sides of the state line. In the 1990s, cities on both sides of the state line agreed (active, passive) to a bi-state sales tax to be used to renovate Kansas City, Missouri's Union Station. Advocates said (active, passive) the new station would bring (active, passive) in tourism that would benefit both sides of the state line. Opponents claimed (active, passive) Kansas City, Missouri, was just trying to dip (active, passive) into the pockets of the more affluent suburbs on the Kansas side. In the end, a compromise was reached (active, passive). The bi-state sales tax was passed (active, passive), but all contributing cities had (active, passive) a say in its use and the tax had (active, passive) a 5-year duration. It was not renewed (active, passive).

Write a brief paragraph with at least five sentences in which you appropriately use three or more active verbs and appropriately use two or more passive verbs. Underline the active verbs once and the passive verbs twice. You may want to write about American inventions that interest you.

_____

_____

_____

_____

_____

_____

_____

_____

17e. Verb Mood

Some of the verbs in the following paragraph are declarative (express a fact), some are subjunctive (express some doubt or something contrary to fact), and some are imperative (express a command). Underline the mood used for each.

Singles bars and dating services are thriving (declarative, subjunctive, imperative), but there are always new approaches. In commercial dating services, one new approach that may be cheaper (declarative, subjunctive, imperative) than the standard videotaped interviews is the lunch-date service. For less than $50 a month, the company promises (declarative, subjunctive, imperative) three lunch dates a month. People are paired on the basis of simple criteria gathered from brief interviews that might last (declarative, subjunctive, imperative) less than five minutes. The company sets up the lunch date, and the participants take it from there. "Meet (declarative, subjunctive, imperative) new people," says the advertising brochure, "and enjoy (declarative, subjunctive, imperative) some interesting little restaurants." Since the Census Bureau puts (declarative, subjunctive, imperative) the number of single adults at 66 million and growing, these new twists on dating services may prosper (declarative, subjunctive, imperative).

Write sentences using each of the verb moods listed below.

1. declarative

_____

_____

2. subjunctive

_____

_____

3. imperative

_____

_____

17f. Modal Verbs

The following paragraph includes modal verbs that express ability, a request, or an attitude (such as interest, expectation, possibility, or obligation). Underline the correct meaning from the choices given in parentheses after the modal verbs.

When American products began appearing in Moscow, city officials worried that the signs and advertising for these products might make (intend to make, could possibly make, need to make) Moscow look less Russian. A law recently passed in Moscow warns that all stores and businesses must display (are capable of displaying, expect to display, need to display) signs in Russian or at least change them into the Cyrillic alphabet. This has caused many businesses to contact the city inspector because of questions they have. For example, one businessman wondered whether he should change (has the ability to change, asks to change, is obliged to change) the letters in the label for the Puma running shoes that he sells. He was concerned that changing the letters from English to Russian might make (has the possibility of making, intends to make, requests to make) the shoes less well-known. The problem became confusing because the new law does not forbid foreign words but does require the Russian sign to be bigger than the one in English. Different stores found different solutions. An American cosmetics company, Esteé Lauder, announced that they will put (are capable of putting, strongly intend to put, are asking permission to put) one sign with the Russian alphabet on their awning and another sign with the English alphabet in the windows. Despite all the questions and worries, the inspector in charge of enforcing this rule will be very strict about checking on foreign signs.

Write a brief paragraph with at least five sentences in which you use four or five modal verbs (shall, should, will, would, can, could, may, might, must, ought to). Underline each modal verb that you use. You may want to write about problems in translating words from one language to another or about the difficulties of having to use the English alphabet to write words from a language that uses a different alphabet.

_____

_____

_____

_____

_____

_____

_____

_____

Chapter 18

Nouns and Pronouns

18a. Nouns

In the following paragraph, make the necessary corrections to the nouns that need the appropriate -s and -es plural noun endings and to the nouns that are missing possessive markers. Underline your corrections.

Sports fanatics are spending large sums of money these day to purchase sports memorabilia. In fact, says one of the industrys spokesperson, it is a $100 million-a-year obsession. Buyers look for scorecards, stadium seats, autographed baseball bats, and even children clothing that belonged to old-time greats such as Babe Ruth. Ruth personal letter to a fan recently sold for over $7000. Since Joe Lewis, the famous boxer, kept many of his old mouthpiece, collector are paying over $2000 for boxed sets of Lewis's mouthpieces. There is even a magazine entitled *Sports Collectors Digest* which keeps collector informed about many of the auction and the availability of various item of interest. A faculty member in the history department of a major American university has begun a study of this phenomenon and reports that yearly increases in prices are staggering. For example, he says, a nineteenth-century baseball card of an obscure Hall of Fame pitcher, Tim O'Keefe, which was worth about $750 two year ago, recently sold for over $30,000. O'Keefes other memorabilia are expected to soar in value as well. Sports collectible are now big business.

Write a paragraph of at least five sentences and include nouns with -s and -es plural endings and nouns with correct possessive markers. Underline each such noun that you use. You may want to write about collecting sports memorabilia.

_____

_____

_____

_____

_____

_____

_____

_____

_____

18b. Pronouns

In the following paragraph, underline all the pronouns, including the personal pronouns, demonstrative pronouns, relative pronouns, interrogative pronouns, indefinite pronouns, possessive pronouns, reflexive pronouns, and reciprocal pronouns.

The business of sports collectibles has become so profitable that it has attracted con artists who manage to forge and sell bogus items. The forgeries have become such big business, in fact, that many con artists help one another and have developed a large network of bogus items. These items include fake Joe DiMaggio signatures and imitation press box pins. Anyone who is in the memorabilia business can spot these forgeries and fakes, but sports fans are often too enthusiastic about a purchase to take the time to have their purchases checked by experts. As a result, they often allow themselves to be conned. A lot of junk from people's attics is also cluttering the market. When someone finds yellowed pages from 1929 sports sections in her scrapbook, she may think she has an expensive treasure. Flea markets overflow with these antiques which may or may not be worth anything. But if a buyer is willing to pay large sums of money, who can say whether that autographed photo or threadbare jersey is or is not a treasure worth collecting? With a market where buyers pay $20,000 for one of Lou Gehrig's old bats, it is worth cleaning out those old attics and scrapbooks.

Chapter 19

Pronoun Case and Reference

19a. Pronoun Case

In the following paragraph, underline the correct pronoun in the parentheses.

When historian Page Smith began to ask himself just what kind of education was being provided by American universities, he started with a list of questions. (His, His') answers can be found in (his, his') book entitled *Killing the Spirit*. (Them, Those) readers looking for encouraging conclusions will not find (they, them) in this report as Smith criticizes professors' lack of interest in teaching and (their, theirs, their') tendency to spend too much time writing books and articles that do not contribute anything useful to mankind's betterment. Smith finds (them, those) academics who look down on teaching as less important than research to be at fault. For (he, him), the student revolt of the 1960s and early 1970s was a time when students were looking for answers to important questions but got no help from their professors. There was no dialogue between their professors and (they, them) that addressed questions about meaning and values in life, says Smith. However, community colleges and small, independent colleges still concern (theirselves, themselves) with the needs of students. University administrators (who, whom) are more interested in budgets and specific agendas will not find answers in Smith's book, and readers will wonder (who, whom) his real audience is. To (who, whom) should (we, us) look for answers?

Write your own sentences below correctly using the pronouns listed.

1. them

   _____

   _____

2. whom

   _____

   _____

3. his

_____

_____

4. yours

_____

_____

5. theirs

_____

_____

6. ours

_____

_____

7. her

_____

_____

8. me

_____

_____

9. who

_____

_____

10. your

_____

_____

11. us

_____

_____

12. I

_____

_____

19b. Pronoun Reference

In the following paragraph there are some pronoun reference problems. Underline all the pronouns that do not clearly or correctly refer back to specific nouns.

When Benjamin Franklin discovered electricity in thunderclouds, he sparked a controversy that still has no clear answer. How do clouds become electrified in the first place? To this day they haven't been able to adequately explain how it contains such incredible amounts of electricity that a stroke of lightning can contain about 100 million volts. One researcher who wants to find some answers flies his plane into storms to measure electric fields and ice particle changes. It's bumpy work, he says, especially if there are large hailstones because it can damage the plane and the measuring equipment. On one trip they noticed that in sections of clouds where water and ice mix, the measuring devices picked up indications of strong charge separation. The answer may be that in a certain temperature range, the temperature can cause the charge separation. Another factor may be a kind of soft hail called "graupel," pea-sized particles that can look like miniature raspberries. They form when droplets of supercooled water collide, freezing together instantly. Ice crystals then bounce off the growing graupel, building up a charge from the friction just as you build up a static electricity charge when you scuff your feet across the carpet. When they are carried to different parts of the cloud, the result is a separation of the positively and negatively charged particles. Then, when the electrical difference between the ground and the sky becomes great enough, everyone should haul his or her kite in.

Write a paragraph of at least five sentences with correctly used pronouns in every sentence. Underline each pronoun and draw an arrow back to the noun to which it refers. You may want to write about electricity or thunderstorms.

_____

61

Chapter 20

Adjective and Adverbs

20a. Adjectives and Adverbs

In the following paragraph, underline all the adjectives and adverbs and correct the errors in adverb and adjective forms.

     For many people, the crossword puzzle in the daily paper is one of life's little pleasures. Some say it is also sure one of life's frustrations. While puzzle books conveniently include the answers in the back, most newspapers print the answers the next day. Now there is a more quicker answer. Some companies have an automated solution. Readers can dial an 800 service for instant answers. This service is free to callers but is paid for by advertisers who sponsor each day's puzzle. An advertiser can run a small advertisement by the puzzle and can include a ten-second message that callers will hear before the answers are given. *The New York Times* handles this more differently. For their puzzles, callers pay for all requests for clues. These services are a major breakthrough for frustrated puzzle-doers who are used to waiting until the next day.

Write sentences correctly using each of the adjectives or adverbs below.

1. nice

   _____

   _____

2. nicely

   _____

   _____

3. sure

   _____

   _____

4. surely

_____

_____

5. used

_____

_____

6. good

_____

_____

7. well

_____

_____

8. rapid

_____

_____

9. rapidly

_____

_____

10. real

_____

_____

11. really

_____

_____

12. so

_____

_____

20b. A, An, The

In the following paragraph, articles (a, an, the) may or may not be needed before certain nouns. Underline the correct answer in parentheses. Notice that one possibility is that no article is needed; if that is the case, underline that option.

After winding down twenty miles of dirt road in Mtunthama, Malawi, (a, an, the, no article) visitors will come upon the well-kept lawns and gardens of (a, an, the, no article) Kamuzu Academy, one of (a, an, the, no article) Africa's most unusual schools. Here, on four hundred acres of well-trimmed lands is (a, an, the, no article) school dedicated to classical scholarship. (A, An, The, no article) school was founded by President Hastings Kamuzu Banda, the ruler of Malawi since it won its independence from (a, an, the, no article) British in 1964. Originally, Dr. Banda studied in (a, an, the, no article) South Africa, (a, an, the, no article) United States of America, and (a, an, the, no article) Britain, where he acquired (a, an, the, no article) medical degree and (a, an, the, no article) love of Latin and Greek, as well as a strong attraction to the classical emphasis of the elite British schools. When Dr. Banda returned to Malawi, he wanted to copy (a, an, the, no article) architecture and curriculum of Eton and other British boarding schools. Some critics in opposition to Dr. Banda say that (a, an, the, no article) academy is not appropriate in their country where ordinary schools often do not have (a, an, the, no article) textbooks and where more than two-thirds of (a, an, the, no article) population are illiterate. However, defenders of the school point out that the school is not elite in choosing its students. Children are accepted without regard to their family's wealth or position. Each year 35,000 students take (a, an, the, no article) exam to try to gain entrance to the school which accepts about eighty new students (a, an, the, no article) year. Once accepted, all students are required to take four years of (a, an, the, no article) Latin and four years of (a, an, the, no article) ancient Greek, along with (a, an, the, no article) English, (a, an, the, no article) mathematics, and (a, an, the, no article) history course about Africa. Most graduates go on to university and then take jobs in (a, an, the, no article) Malawi civil service.

65

20c. Comparisons

Write sentences in which you use the correct comparative form of the word listed for the items given.

1. comparative form: large

   items compared: two colleges

   _____

   _____

2. comparative form: large

   items compared: eight colleges

   _____

   _____

3. comparative form: exciting

   items compared: two movies

   _____

   _____

4. comparative form: enjoyable

   items compared: three books

   _____

   _____

5. comparative form: user-friendly

   items compared: all computer software programs tested

   _____

   _____

6. comparative form: good

   items compared: two music CDs

   _____

   _____

7. comparative form: good

    items compared: three music CDs

    _____

    _____

8. comparative form: bad

    items compared: all meals you have ever eaten

    _____

    _____

Chapter 21

Prepositions

In the following paragraph, underline the correct choice for the preposition that should be used.

Americans used to pour ketchup over so many foods that it was America's favorite condiment. Now salsa has replaced ketchup as the favorite (among, between) the two (at, in, on) American food markets. Salsa, which means "sauce" (at, in, on) Spanish, is defined as any fresh-tasting, chunky mixture, usually made with tomatoes, chilies, onions, and other seasonings. Although salsa used to be associated (to, with, for) Mexican and southwestern cooking, it is being used for a variety of foods not particularly Mexican. The popularity (of, about, to) salsa is apparently part of the current food trend as Americans become more interested (about, on, in) spicier foods. In 1988, only 16 percent of households (at, among, in) America bought salsa. (In, At, For) two years, that figure was up to 36 percent, and the market continues to grow (in, at, by) a very fast rate. A marketing information company notes that salsas and picantes—which are different (from, than) salsas because they are thinner—account (on, to, for) about two-thirds of this market, a category that also includes taco and enchilada sauces. As the market expands, so do the choices. The simplest salsas are based (about, around, on) chopped tomatoes and chilies, and the types of chilies determine how hot the particular type of salsa is. Cookbooks with a variety of recipes indicate the preference of some people to make their salsas (in, at, to) home. Salsas are one of the few popular snack foods that are fat-free or nearly so, and many are made without preservatives, two characteristics that may contribute (on, to, around) their popularity now that people are interested (about, in) eating healthier. Riding on this wave of popularity are the new fruit salsas, made with peaches, pineapples, and so on, and vegetable salsas, made with pinto beans, corn, and black-eyed peas. Other varieties will surely appear as the market expands (in, on, at) the future.

Write sentences in which you correctly use the prepositions listed.

1. compared to

   _____

   _____

2. compared with

_____

_____

3. independent of

_____

_____

4. similar to

_____

_____

5. different from

_____

_____

Chapter 22

Subjects

In the following paragraph, underline the subjects of all the verbs.

Because television viewers of sporting events like to follow the actions of specific players, a cable company in New York is trying out a new subscription service. If it is successful, it is likely to become available to everyone: Cable subscribers will be able to tune into a tournament and pick the player they want to follow. Using a wand similar to a TV remote control, viewers sitting at home will be able to switch from conventional network coverage to a camera that focuses solely on the preferred player. Instant replays and a list of statistics on selected pros will be other selections that the service will provide. This interactive technology will allow viewers to customize programming. While the present programming is only a test of the technology, some cable companies foresee customers being able to sign up for interactive television just like other cable services. When will this service be available for everyone? It is too soon to know for sure, but there is certainly a large demand for such services.

Write a paragraph of five or more sentences and underline the word or words that are the subjects of all the clauses in your sentences. You may want to write about television viewing, cable services, or active vs. passive television viewing.

_____

_____

_____

_____

_____

_____

_____

_____

Chapter 23

Phrases

For each of the following sentences, choose the letter which best indicates the function of the underlined phrase.

    a. subject of the sentence

    b. tells more about the subject

    c. is the verb phrase

    d. gives added information about the verb

    e. completes the subject

    f. gives added information about another element in the sentence

1. Marketers <u>have been working on</u> ways to improve aerosol dispensers so that they do not spray the harmful propellant into the atmosphere.

2. One new product, <u>an alcohol-free hair spray</u>, cuts emissions of chemical pollutants by roughly 60 percent.

3. For its propellant, this new hair spray uses dimethyloxide, a <u>nondamaging chemical</u>.

4. Reformulating a proven compound <u>can be expensive</u> for manufacturers.

5. Another solution to the problem is <u>a propellant-free container</u> with a rubber expanding sleeve.

6. <u>The rubber's propensity to contract</u> provides the pressure to produce a spray when the nozzle is pressed.

7. This new spray dispenser is already being widely used <u>with great success</u>.

Write your own sentences with phrases that serve the functions listed here, and underline the phrases you have used fulfilling those functions.

1. phrase that is the subject of the sentence

    _____

    _____

2. phrase that tells more about the subject

    _____

_____

3. phrase that is the verb phrase

   _____

   _____

4. phrase that gives added information about the verb

   _____

   _____

5. phrase that completes the subject

   _____

   _____

6. phrase that gives added information about another element in the sentence

   _____

   _____

Chapter 24

Clauses

24a. Independent Clauses

In the following paragraph, underline the independent clauses.

     If you are a magician and like highly structured organizations, you may want to join either the International Brotherhood of Magicians or the Society of American Magicians. If, however, you are a magician who lives in New York City and likes to gather informally with other magicians, you should visit Reuben's Restaurant on 38th Street and Madison Avenue any Saturday afternoon. There will be professional and amateur magicians sitting in the back room, and they will be swapping tricks or polishing their routines on each other. People come in with jumbo interlocking rings, decks of cards, and brightly colored scarves in their pockets. Some are doctors, professors, salespersons in shoe stores, tax attorneys, shipping clerks, or teenagers who are just learning the basics. Others are professionals who have appeared on *The Tonight Show* or in traveling circuses. They all share a love of magic, and they willingly sit and watch each other's routines because they know how valuable it is to keep practicing.

Write a paragraph with at least five sentences in which at least four sentences have more than one independent clause. Underline the independent clauses you use. You may want to write about magicians or magic.

_____

_____

_____

_____

_____

_____

_____

_____

_____

_____

24b. Dependent Clauses

In the following paragraph, underline the dependent clauses and identify them as adjective or adverb clauses.

There are an estimated 50,000 magicians in America. Most are amateurs who enjoy magic as a hobby. These amateurs often have elaborate equipment although their only audience is usually their friends and relatives. Some, however, specialize in the small card, coin, and rope tricks that are always popular. Purists call this intimate "close-up" magic the only real magic because it relies so heavily on a person's manual dexterity. Because people seem to prefer to be fooled face-to-face, this close-up magic is also offered by professional magicians who perform at birthday parties and trade shows. A psychologist who is also a magician says that when something is done under people's noses, it's more magical. It's much more elusive. The spectacular effects of magic done on television don't seem to impress people quite so much. Whatever the cause may be, amateur magicians will keep buying those sponge balls, decks of cards, special coins, and paper flowers.

Write a paragraph of at least five sentences in which three or more sentences have dependent clauses. Underline the dependent clauses. You may want to write about magic or magicians.

_____

_____

_____

_____

_____

_____

_____

_____

_____

_____

Chapter 25

Essential and Nonessential Clauses and Phrases

Rewrite the following paragraph so that all the nonessential clauses and phrases are taken out of the sentence and put in a new sentence following the one they are in now. Identify the essential clauses by underlining them.

Music teachers in the elementary schools who want to teach classical music to their students now have a lot of materials to help them. The materials, which many students say are excellent, have been developed by a group of educators who want to introduce classical music appreciation programs in elementary schools. These programs, incorporating listening skills and information about themes, styles, and forms of music, are also being used to coach students for contests. Students seem to enjoy these contests, a new form of competition in many schools. Contestants are often asked to identify the main themes of familiar works such as *Nutcracker Suite*, the specific instruments being played, and the composers. Harder questions, ones that stump even the more experienced teams, are those that are asked about music the students have not studied in school. Not all the music that is studied in the music appreciation classes is classical. Sometimes jazz and non-Western music is added, though students also seem to enjoy studying classical music that they have heard on television commercials. Music teachers who have tried these programs are pleased with the variety of types of music students come to like and the quantity of music they come to know. These music appreciation programs, begun on a small scale in a few states, are expanding rapidly across the nation.

Write a paragraph of at least five sentences in which at least three sentences have an essential clause and at least two sentences have nonessential clauses. Underline the nonessential clauses. You may want to write about studying music in school.

_____

_____

_____

_____

_____

_____

_____

_____

Chapter 26

Sentences

Identify each of the following sentences according to the letter which describes it.

    a. simple sentence (one independent clause)

    b. compound sentence (two or more independent clauses)

    c. complex sentence (at least one independent clause and at least one dependent clause)

    d. compound-complex sentence (at least two independent clauses and at least one dependent clause)

    e. incomplete sentence (does not have at least one independent clause)

1. In today's society many working people who are in their thirties or forties face the problem of providing care for both their children and elderly parents while they are at work.

2. Since children have less contact with older people than in previous generations, a growing number of programs are being designed to bring children and older people together.

3. Which will benefit both groups.

4. In some programs there are centers for child care next to centers for the elderly, and there are plenty of opportunities for visiting between the centers.

5. Including shared activities such as cooking and birthday parties and informal get-togethers for storytelling hours.

6. Psychologists point out that this kind of contact, even between old people and youngsters who are not related, can fill a void in young children's lives when they do not have a grandparent living near by.

7. In addition, companionship with children keeps older people from feeling isolated and lonely.

8. There is also a societal need for older people to transmit life experiences to younger generations.

9. Something that is becoming increasingly less frequent in our mobile society where children move away from their parents and raise families on their own.

10. Programs to link children and the elderly have been so successful that similar programs have also sprung up that link retirees with at-risk teenagers, and these programs are providing great benefits to the teenagers.

11. A group based in Washington, D.C., which is a coalition of national organizations representing old and young constituents, works to push goals of mutual interest to the two age groups.

Write sentences illustrating each of the following types of sentences.

1. compound sentence

   _____

   _____

2. simple sentence

   _____

   _____

3. incomplete sentence

   _____

   _____

4. complex sentence

   _____

   _____

5. compound-complex sentence

   _____

   _____

PART FOUR
PUNCTUATION

Chapter 27

Commas

27a. Commas in Compound Sentences

The following paragraph contains some compound sentences that need commas. Add commas where they are needed, and underline each comma you have added.

In 1977 the flight of the little airplane, the Gossamer Condor, did not look very impressive but it was indeed a historic flight. With wings of foam, balsa wood, and Mylar, the plane designed by Paul MacCready floated slowly and gracefully over the San Joaquin Valley and covered a mile or so in about eight minutes. What made it so historic was that the pilot was pedaling. The Gossamer Condor was only the first of MacCready's pedal-powered planes and two years later the plane's successor, the Gossamer Albatross, crossed the English Channel. Some people say that MacCready is really the brains behind these inventions but others feel that he receives undue credit for the work that others on the development teams do. However, MacCready was the first to use his observations of how birds fly so his supporters feel that he is the genius who made human-powered flight possible. Other inventors were taking the conventional approach of trying to reduce drag as much as possible because they thought this approach would be the answer. The approaches of other inventors were to streamline their aircraft or they tried to incorporate ways to increase the horsepower. Only MacCready applied the principle of vastly increasing the wing area and used materials to keep the overall weight down. The result was an aircraft that needed only the power output of a good bicyclist and the Gossamer Condor now has a place of honor next to the *Spirit of St. Louis* in the Smithsonian Institute's National Air and Space Museum.

Write a paragraph with at least five compound sentences that are punctuated correctly with commas. You may want to write about the development of the airplane.

_____

_____

_____

_____

_____

_____

_____

_____

_____

27b. Commas After Introductory Words, Phrases, and Clauses

The following paragraph contains some sentences with introductory words, phrases, and clauses that need commas. Add commas where they are needed, and underline each comma you have added.

Having won prizes with his first human-powered plane Paul MacCready went on to build a faster and more powerful pedal-powered plane, the Gossamer Albatross. In less than two years after his first success MacCready's second pedal-powered plane departed from Folkestone, England, in June, 1979, bound for France. Expecting the flight to take about two hours MacCready allotted just enough water for the pilot to drink. The flight team who prepared the plane and assisted the pilot on the ground waited several weeks for the kind of calm weather that was needed. Consequently the pilot took off, expecting to reach France before his endurance and the water gave out. But a head wind blew up soon after the pilot was aloft. An hour and a half later he was only two-thirds of the way to France, and his legs were cramping from all the pedaling. Because everyone was sure they had to give up the attempt the flight team was ready to hook a towline to the craft that would haul it ashore. Tired and about to give up the pilot knew he had to gain altitude to get hooked to the towline. As he climbed he found less wind and was able to press on. Almost three hours later the pilot touched down at Cape Gris-Nez, in France, a minute short of his theoretical exhaustion point. The Gossamer Albatross had crossed the English Channel, powered only by the pilot.

Write a paragraph with at least five sentences that have introductory words, phrases, and clauses correctly punctuated with commas. You may want to write about a strenuous sport or competiton you were in.

27c. Commas with Essential and Nonessential Words, Phrases, and Clauses

The following paragraph contains some sentences with essential words, phrases, and clauses that need commas. Add commas where they are needed, and underline the commas you have added.

      After designing human-powered planes, Paul MacCready a prize-winning inventor went on to design a solar-powered plane. MacCready however realized that solar cells as an energy source for planes do not make any practical sense. But MacCready who had long sympathized with environmental concerns hoped to demonstrate that solar power has an important part in the world's energy future. Those who see solar energy as merely a minor source of energy for the future downplay the importance of such demonstrations. Others think solar power has simply not been adequately developed for practical use. The solar-powered plane that MacCready designed flew from Paris to the coast of England in 1981 cruising at 441 mph at an altitude of 11,000 feet. The plane called the Solar Challenger provided the stepping stone to MacCready's next flying machine the Sunraycer a solar-powered car.

Write a paragraph with at least five sentences that contain essential and nonessential words, phrases, and clauses correctly punctuated with commas. You may want to write about the future of solar energy.

81

_____

_____

_____

_____

_____

_____

_____

27d–h. Commas in Series and Lists; Commas with Adjectives; Commas with Dates, Addresses, Geographical Names, and Numbers; Other Uses for Commas; Unnecessary Commas

The following paragraph contains some sentences with correct comma usage and with some comma errors. Add commas where they are needed, omit unneeded or incorrect commas, and underline each change you make.

The Sunraycer which is a solar-powered lightweight car, was built to compete in the 1987 Race Across Australia. Designed by Paul MacCready the car won the race from Darwin to Adelaide, and is now in the Smithsonian Institute's National Museum of American History. With a total weight of 365 pounds the car has a power output of about 1.8 horsepower at noon on a bright day and it gets the electric power equivalent of 500 miles to the gallon. The Sunraycer which presently holds the solar-powered speed record of 48.7 mph averaged a little over 40 mph for much of the race. The car is so light, that when it made turns during testing it often seemed in danger of blowing over. The engineers who worked on the Sunraycer, ended up putting two little ears on the top. "We're not sure why they work" said one engineer "though they seem to help." In some ways the Sunraycer is not a prototype of electric cars for commercial use, because the Sunraycer has bicycle-thin wheels a driver's seat that requires the driver to lay flat, and very weak acceleration. However many of Sunraycer's features were carried over into the electric car developed by General Motors. Like the Sunraycer the GM car uses alternating current, and can therefore get better performance. If electric-powered cars become widely popular in the future Paul MacCready will feel that he had some small part in saving the environment.

Chapter 28

Apostrophes

The following paragraph contains sentences with some apostrophes incorrectly used to show possession, mark contractions, and indicate plurals, as well as some missing apostrophes. Add apostrophes where they are needed (even if they are optional), omit those that are unneeded or incorrect, and underline each change you make.

In the game of baseball, batting slump's are one of a players worst nightmares. When they are doing well, player's attribute their successes to mysterious minor occurrences around them that then become habits' the players keep up. After a game in which one baseball player who was wearing an old helmet with it's side dented hit two triple's, a home run, and a single, the player continued to wear that helmet for the rest of the season. Warding off evil spirits through superstitions is another thing baseball player's do. One player always wears the green T-shirt from his university under his teams jersey. Another wont wear a jersey with any 6s in his players number. Batting coaches spend hours watching videotapes with slumping players, trying to find whats causing the problem. They examine the players batting stance or swing, but this does'nt always provide useful clues. Some slumps happen when batters begin to worry too much about their misses and about everyone elses successes. But one coach thinks otherwise. He notes that some players' start making adjustments when theyve hit a double and want to hit farther or when a certain unusual pitch connected well with their bats. Players in their 30s' complain of a different kind of slump. One bad day, says one over-30 player, may mean he is losing it, that his age has begun to take it's toll. A hitter who is hot, on the other hand, tends to get possessive about a special bat and uses it until it breaks or its' cracks begin to show. When that bat goes, the player sometimes loses confidence until he connects with a new bat that brings him a few homerun's. A batters life is'nt as easy as some people think it is.

Write a paragraph with at least five sentences that use apostrophes correctly. You may want to write about the performance slumps of professional athletes or teams or about low periods or slumps in your life.

_____

_____

_____

_____

_____

Chapter 29

Semicolons

The following paragraph contains some sentences that need semicolons and some sentences with incorrectly used semicolons. Add or change punctuation marks to semicolons where they are needed, delete those that are incorrect, and add correct punctuation, if needed. Underline each change you make.

Junk mail used to be confined to print on paper, now it is appearing in people's mailboxes on videocassettes. Companies in the direct-mail business are now marketing inexpensive cardboard videocassettes that can carry a variety of messages; such as audiovisual advertisements, promotional premiums, and educational or training aids. Some companies are switching to this form of direct-mail advertising because it is relatively cheap, in addition, it presents messages more vividly on television screens than print advertising can on paper. Informational videos can be sent to prospective customers, and advertisers can use their product in the video. Says the spokesperson for one cereal company, "We are interested in promoting good nutritional habits;" as might be expected, the balanced diet they will be picturing in the video will include their cereal. Printed instructions in merchandise are often confusing, consequently, some manufacturers are also switching to these disposable videocassettes for the instructional packets they include with their merchandise. The cardboard videocassettes are relatively cheap to manufacture and cheap to mail. They are certainly more convenient than the promotional packets sent by companies that have relied on enclosing sample packets of toothpaste, aspirin, or cereal, mail advertisers who send bulky envelopes of coupons, and companies who want to entice customers with big brochures of vacation places, hotels, and tours. The disposable videocassette is certainly going to grow in popularity as an advertising medium.

Write a paragraph with at least five sentences that use semicolons in compound sentences and lists. You may want to write about junk mail.

_____

_____

_____

_____

_____

_____

Chapter 30

Colons

The following paragraph contains some sentences that need colons and some sentences with incorrectly used colons. Add or change punctuation marks to colons where they are needed, delete those that are incorrect, and add correct punctuation, if needed. Underline each change you make.

Evaluating college teachers is a complex, often difficult task. Now a new method devised in the Midwest is being tried out across the nation the teaching portfolio. Administrators and faculty members see the portfolio, a collection of materials documenting classroom performance, as a way to emphasize teaching as a major priority. Too often, professors who are being evaluated document primarily their research and scholarly activities, such as: published books and article, lists of grants, and conference presentations. Says one faculty member at a large Eastern university, "When it comes to teaching, most teachers only have student evaluations and coffee-room conversations about what they do in class and how their students are learning": this kind of evidence is not very thorough or sufficient to determine pay raises, tenure, and promotion. As a result, many faculty members are judged and rewarded on the basis of their research and publications. Their teaching performance, whether outstanding or mediocre, is largely ignored. The portfolio can be a better measure of what faculty really do as teachers, for the portfolio can consist of the following items: a statement of the person's teaching philosophy, a list of the courses that person has taught, a representative syllabus, statements by fellow faculty members who have observed this person, and course materials that the person has prepared. At some schools where portfolios are already in use, the portfolios also include: unsolicited letters from former students, teaching awards, and even videotapes of the candidate teaching a class. Some faculty members who have prepared these portfolios say that there is an added advantage, the portfolio collection can lead to self-improvement. This can happen when the process of creating the collection causes the person to think seriously about teaching goals, strategies, and results.

Write sentences using colons in each of the patterns below.

1. Colon to announce an element at the end of the sentence

   _____

   _____

2. Colon to separate independent clauses

_____

_____

3. Colon to announce a long quotation

_____

_____

4. Colon in a salutation

_____

_____

5. Colon between elements

_____

_____

6. Colon with quotation marks

_____

_____

Chapter 31

Quotation Marks

The following paragraph contains some sentences with correct and incorrect use of quotation marks. Revise and add quotation marks, if needed. Underline each change you make.

"Why am I fatter than my sister-in-law? I eat less, complained a woman being studied by a team of researchers. She explained that she "repeatedly went on diets when her sister-in-law didn't." But the woman continues to weigh more. Researchers are finding out that heredity, in addition to "lifestyle," exerts a strong influence on people's weight. By studying identical and fraternal twins, research teams are finding that brothers and sisters end up with similar body weights whether or not they are raised in different families. In the "Journal of Genetics," Dr. Albert Skinnerd writes, "When the biological parents are fat, there is an 80 percent chance that their children will also be overweight". (234). "Does this mean that my brother and I are doomed to be fat," asked one overweight twin in the study? Since some sets of twins tend to transform extra calories into fat while other sets of twins tend to convert extra calories into muscle, one scientist concluded that "genes do seem to have something to do with the amount you gain when you overeat". Some unsuccessful dieters may be relieved to know that their failed diets aren't a matter of failed "willpower." It is really a matter of metabolism", reports another doctor doing research in this field. But that does not mean that low-fat diets and exercise should be given up. Quit is not a word in my vocabulary", says one constant dieter who manages to maintain a reasonable weight by means of careful eating and plenty of exercise, despite a tendency to be overweight.

Write a paragraph with at least five sentences using at least five sets of quotation marks for direct quotations, minor titles and parts of wholes, words used as words, and other uses of quotation marks. You may want to write about dieting.

Chapters 32, 33, 34

Hyphens, End Punctuation, and Other Punctuation

The following paragraph needs one or more hyphens, dashes, slashes, parentheses, and brackets. Add those that are needed, revise any that are not used correctly, and underline all changes that you make.

Which oils are good for us to eat? A study of thirty nine participants on a reduced fat diet looked at the benefits of consuming olive oil and [or] corn oil. Which is more beneficial in influencing high/density lipoprotein levels corn oil or olive oil? This is an important question because high-density lipoprotein [HDL] is considered a beneficial form of cholesterol that helps remove the more dangerous low—density lipoproteins from the body. In a study published in an article, "Two Healthy Oils for Human Consumption" [*Diet and Health News* 14 (1991): 22–36], researchers report that the participants first spent twelve weeks on a diet that included olive-oil and then another twelve weeks on a corn oil diet. The results (which were also announced on television newscasts) indicated that neither diet resulted in lower-levels of HDL. This indicates that a diet of olive oil and (or) corn oil can accompany a reduced—fat diet. For those who self-select the oils they use in their diet, the choice is probably a matter of taste-or cost.

The following paragraph contains some sentences with incorrect use of periods, question marks, exclamation points, and ellipses. Add or change these punctuation marks where they are needed, delete those that are incorrect, and add correct punctuation, if needed. Underline each change you make.

"Do you see that green area to the left of the river we are flying over"? said the pilot to the passengers as the commercial 747 jet flew over southern Texas. Continued the pilot, "That's my grandfather's ranch! I often visited there as a kid!" Public address systems in commercial planes are now being used by pilots to enliven their passengers' flights. Some pilots are opposed to this practice because they see it as a distraction. Says one seasoned veteran, "Our task......is to fly the plane, not amuse the passengers". But others disagree. Interesting, informative comments can put nervous passengers more at ease and can shorten a long flight. For those pilots interested in making such public-address announcements, there is now a book put together by an ex-pilot which pinpoints more than 1,200 historical and little-known places of interest on a collection of highway maps of the U.S. The maps are overlaid with the flight paths used by commercial pilots. Are you flying between El Paso, Texas, and Las Vegas, New Mexico. If so, then look for the site of the Berringer Crater, where a meteor hit with such force 22,000 years ago that it killed all animal and plant life within 100 miles! Thousands of these maps have been sold, with more frequent fliers than pilots doing the buying! "We are learning...an awful lot about territory we thought we knew"! says one frequent flier who takes her book with her on every flight. Another customer reports, "I bought one for my uncle who hates airplanes, and he now actually enjoys his flights". The book is obviously a success! Is the author correct when he says, "Soon, there will be such books in the pocket of every seat in every commercial flight?"

Write a paragraph with at least five sentences correctly using one hyphen, one dash, one slash, one ellipsis, one set of parentheses, and one set of brackets. Also use three different kinds of end punctuation correctly. You may want to write about commercial flights.

_____

_____

_____

_____

_____

_____

_____

_____

PART FIVE

MECHANICS AND SPELLING

Chapters 35, 36, 37

Capitals, Abbreviations, and Numbers

Revise the following paragraph for correct use of capitals and abbreviations, as well as the correct way to write numbers. Underline all changes that you make.

One of Boston's most popular folk heroes is Paul Revere, whose Midnight ride was made famous in Longfellow's

poem, "Paul Revere's Ride," in *Tales Of A Wayside Inn*. Not many tourists realize that many of the places mentioned

in that poem are still part of Boston's Twentieth-Century landscape, along what is commonly called the Freedom trail.

This well-marked Trail is actually a 2-mile line in red paint, bricks, or steps with 21 historic buildings, sites, and

monuments documenting Boston's contribution to American history. 2 miles isn't long, but it usually takes tourists

who are thorough 2 or 3 days to see everything on the trail. Most begin at the Boston common, the oldest public park

in the U.S. Here colonists used the public land for grazing animals, training the militia, and staging Public executions.

Immediately next to the Common is America's first public botanical garden, the Boston Public garden, famous partly

because it was the setting for the well-known children's book, *Make Way For Ducklings*. Just across the Street, on

Beacon Street, is another of Boston's famous sites, the Old State House, completed in Seventeen Ninety-Eight. Its

cornerstone was laid by Samuel Adams in 1793. 1 block East on Beacon street and then 1 block south on Park street is

the historic Park street Church on the corner of Tremont. Here the song "America" was first sung on July 4, 1831. The

next stop on the Freedom Trail is the Granary burying Ground, a Cemetery on Tremont Street. Some of the greatest

U.S. patriots, including Paul Revere, Samuel Adams, John Hancock, James Otis, etc, are buried here. Also along

Tremont street, at the corner of School street, is King's Chapel, the first anglican church in Boston. After the

revolution, it became the first unitarian church in the country, and its cemetery contains the graves of many other early

notables, including William Dawes, Jr. and Gov John Winthrop. (it was Gov. Winthrop who headed the group that founded the Boston colony.) Also on School Street is the first public school in america, which later became the Boston public latin School. Rev Cotton Mather, Ralph Waldo Emerson, John Hancock, Benjamin Franklin, et al, were alumni of this School. These are only a few of the many sights along the Freedom Trail. Longfellow's poem says, "hardly a man is now alive who remembers that famous night and ride...." True, but the Freedom Trail helps visitors realize many of the events that led to our Nation's independence.

Write a paragraph with at least five sentences correctly using capitals and numbers. Also include abbreviations of numbers, measurements, and dates. You may want to write about history.

_____

_____

_____

_____

_____

_____

_____

_____

_____

Chapter 38

Underlining/Italics

Listed here are titles and words that either need underlines (or italics) or quotation marks. In the right-hand column, write a "U" if the titles or words need an underline (or italics) or "Q" if the titles or words need quotation marks.

1. Newsweek (magazine)   U
   _____

2. Gone with the Wind (movie)
   _____

3. My Next Adventure (book chapter)
   _____

4. Buffy the Vampire Slayer (TV series)
   _____

5. Moby Dick (book)
   _____

6. To His Coy Mistress (short poem)
   _____

7. The Case of the Lost Diamond (TV episode)
   _____

8. The Barber of Seville (opera)
   _____

9. Paradise Lost (long poem)
   _____

10. Copenhagen's Museums (magazine article)
    _____

11. Time (news magazine)
    _____

12. Sweet Birdie (song)
    _____

13. Civil Rights Revisited (pamphlet)
    _____

14. The Economics of Solar Energy (magazine article)
    _____

15. C (letter of the alphabet)
    _____

16. Jurassic Park (book)
    _____

17. Exxon Valdez (ship)
    _____

18. de jure (Latin phrase)
    _____

19. My Nervous Childhood (essay)   _____

20. Washington Post (newspaper)   _____

Write a paragraph with at least five sentences in which you correctly use underlining at least five times. You may want to write about books, magazines, articles, television programs, and movies that you enjoy.

_____

_____

_____

_____

_____

_____

_____

_____

_____

Chapter 39

Spelling

39a. Proofreading

Proofread the following paragraph for spelling errors, typos, and omitted words. Use the dictionary if needed, and underline all the revisions you make.

Inventors of gadgets for automobiles havn't always been successful with there inventions. But we can see from some these inventions that people have been looking for ways to make cars more functional, better looking, and more fun to drive. for example, we now have elegent and sophisticated ways tohere music in ou cars, but some of the earlier ways to add music to driving seem a bit odd now. In the 1920's, Daniel Young recieved a patent for an organ he invented for use in automobiles. He built organ keyboards that could be attached to back of the front seat so that people ridding in the back could play the organ to entertain themselfs. This may have been a good idea, exept for one thing. The roads of that time, unfortunatly, were so bumpy and uneven that the sounds producted by the organ when the car was moving where anythhing but beautiful. Another terriffic idea that didn't make it was Leander Pelton's patent for a car that could be parked by standing it on end. Instead of a back bumpper, he buildt a vertical platform with rolers attached. When parking the Vertical-Park Car, the driver needed to tip the car back onto platform. Than he could just shove the car into any approrpiately sized space. To preform this task, however, was a big dificult as Pelton never quite explained how the car was to be tiped from horzontal to vertical and back down again. A diffrent problem was that Pelton didn't porvide any way to keep gasoline, water, and oil from spilling once the car was up on its parkking rollers. But the government gave him a patent; he simply couldn't get anyone to manifacture his Vertical-Park car. Another invention that never made it was designed by Joseph Grant in 1926—an autombile wash machine. The machin didn't wash cars, but it suppossedly washed clothes. Grant's invention consistted of a tub and paddles that bolted to the car's runing boards. when the tub was filled with water, soap, and drity clothes, the bouncing of the car over rought roads provided all the power and agitatition necessary to clean a load of dirty clothes. For realy dirty load, an extra twenty miles or so of driving was reccommended.

39c. Some Spelling Guidelines

39c. (1) IE/EI

Using the rules for IE/EI spellings (and the exceptions), underline the correctly spelled words in these sentences.

1. Does he really (beleive, believe) he will win the lottery?

2. The soybean (yeild, yield) this year will be high.

3. She knows how to (seize, sieze) the day.

4. The (height, hieght) of that tree is unusual.

5. The company is working hard to establish more (foreign, foriegn) markets.

6. My (weird, wierd) brother is always trying some crazy new herbal diet.

7. What is your (field, feild) of study?

8. No more than (eight, ieght) people can fit in that van.

9. He tried to (deceive, decieve) himself into thinking he was able to do that.

10. She approached a (financeir, financier) to help her start a new business.

11. We called off the party when (neither, niether) of the guests of honor could come to it.

12. During the rainstorm, the (ceiling, cieling) leaked badly.

13. When is your (neice, niece) coming to visit?

14. Our new (neighbor, nieghbor) seems like a pleasant person.

15. The nurse tried to find a (vein, vien).

39c. (2) Doubling Consonants

Underline the correctly spelled word in these sentences.

1. I have to be quiet when my sister is (naping, napping).

98

2. It was hard to keep my (footing, footting) on that slippery slope.

3. Was that the movie that Paul Newman (starred, stared) in?

4. As she listened to the music, she kept (tapping, taping) her fingers on the desk.

5. To whom were you (writting, writing) that long letter last night?

6. I hope she (referred, refered) me to a good dentist.

7. When I stubbed my toe, I (hopped, hoped) around moaning and complaining.

8. It was a strange (occurrence, occurence) to see the sky lit up like that.

9. I came in at the (begining, beginning) of the movie.

10. They really (benefited, benefitted) from that study session before the exam.

11. My father hates to go (shoping, shopping) when he's on vacation.

12. The advertisement (omitted, omited) any mention of the price.

Use the -ed or -ing forms of the words listed here in sentences.

1. shop

   _____

   _____

2. hope

   _____

   _____

3. tape

   _____

   _____

4. star

_____

_____

5. write

_____

_____

6. top

_____

_____

7. slip

_____

_____

8. omit

_____

_____

9. prefer

_____

_____

10. refer

_____

_____

11. benefit

_____

_____

12.occur

_____

_____

39c. (3) Prefixes and Suffixes

Correctly add the prefixes or suffixes to the words listed here, and then write a sentence using the word and its prefix or suffix. Consult a dictionary if needed to check on the spelling or the meaning of the word that is formed by adding the prefix or suffix.

1. actual + ly

    _____

    _____

2. ante + cedent

    _____

    _____

3. anti + biotic

    _____

    _____

4. auto + biography

    _____

5. bene + diction

_____

_____

6. bi + partisan

_____

_____

7. desire + able

_____

_____

8. de + value

_____

_____

9. dis + agree

_____

_____

10. im + migrate

_____

_____

11. inter + mission

_____

_____

12. mis + inform

_____

_____

13. mis + spell

_____

_____

14. notice + able

_____

_____

15. pre + form

_____

_____

16. per + form

_____

_____

17. picnic + ing

_____

_____

18. pro + nounce

_____

_____

19. real + ly

_____

_____

20. true + ly

39c (4) Y to I

Correctly add the suffixes given to the words listed here, and then write a sentence using the newly formed word.

1. ready + ed

_____

_____

2. lonely + ness

_____

_____

3. carry + ed

_____

_____

4. carry + ing

_____

_____

5. bounty + ful

_____

_____

6. greasy + ness

_____

_____

7. play + ed

_____

_____

8. employ + ed

_____

_____

9. petty + ness

_____

_____

10. forty + eth

_____

_____

39d. Plurals

For each of the following words write a sentence using the plural form of the word.

1. apology

_____

_____

2. ceremony

_____

_____

3. box

_____

_____

4. city

_____

_____

5. sister-in-law

_____

_____

6. church

_____

_____

7. videocassette recorder

_____

_____

8. radio

_____

_____

9. basis

_____

_____

10. attorney

_____

_____

39e. Sound-Alike Words (homonyms)

Underline the correct word in these sentences.

1. Everyone came to the concert (accept, except) Tiana.

2. Does that store (accept, except) personal checks?

3. I think the horror movie he saw (affected, effected) his sleep.

4. The horror movie had no (affect, effect) on him whatsoever.

5. When her friend is visiting (hear, here), she never gets any studying done.

6. (It's, Its) a cool, rainy day today.

7. I wonder when (it's, its) going to get better.

8. What is (it's, its) temperature?

9. Last week (passed, past) so quickly, it seems.

10. She is no bigger (then, than) I am.

11. Leah stayed until her friend joined her, but (then, than) she left the party.

12. What did they do (than, then)?

13. All the speakers (there, their) vowed (there, their) loyalty to the union.

14. I gave my red sweater (to, too) my sister since I have (to, too) many.

15. They (were, where) on the right road, but they took the wrong turn.

16. I never know (whose, who's) right in those arguments.

17. Kristen knows (your, you're) right, but she will never say it to (your, you're) face.

18. Could you give me some (advice, advise) about (buying, bying) a used car?

19. That is going to be the (sight, site, cite) for the new shopping mall.

20. She was (quite, quiet, quit) sure that she had taken her wallet out of her purse.

21. You have to keep the camera (stationary, stationery) when you take the picture.

22. Everyone had (all ready, already) left when the music finally began.

23. I guess it's (alright, all right) to charge that sweater to my mother's account.

24. Perhaps you can use (anyone, any one) of the golf balls lying there.

25. The kit to build that model comes (altogether, all together) with the tools you will need.

Use the following words in sentences. Be sure that they are spelled correctly.

1. accept

_____

_____

2. except

_____

_____

3. affect

_____

_____

4. effect

_____

_____

5. here

_____

_____

6. hear

_____

_____

7. its

_____

_____

8. it's

_____

_____

9. passed

_____

_____

10. past

_____

_____

11. than

_____

_____

12. then

_____

_____

13. they're

_____

_____

14. their

_____

_____

15. there

_____

_____

16. too

_____

_____

17. to

_____

_____

18. were

_____

_____

19. we're

_____

_____

20. where

_____

_____

21. who's

_____

_____

22. whose

_____

_____

23. your

_____

_____

24. you're

_____

_____

25. advice

_____

_____

26. advise

_____

_____

27. site

_____

_____

28. cite

_____

_____

29. sight

_____

_____

30. dessert

_____

_____

31. desert

_____

_____

PART SIX
STYLE AND WORD CHOICE

Chapter 40

Sexist Language

The following paragraph has some sexist language that can be revised. Rewrite the paragraph so that sexist language has been eliminated, and underline all the changes that you make. You may need to make other changes in various sentences as well.

In many suburban housing developments built during recent decades there are homeowners associations that enforce housing codes on all the homeowners. The average owner in such a suburb may think that he is free to paint his house whatever color he likes or park any kind of car in his driveway, but that is not the case. Homeowners associations often have a lawyer who spends his days enforcing the laws enacted by these associations. The laws see to it that all the members abide by the group's standards of good taste. No plastic flamingos are allowed on the lawn, and every house painter who works in the suburb knows that he cannot use certain colors for house trim, such as bright pink or a gaudy yellow, because he has to follow community guidelines. When houses are built in new developments, there are usually restrictive covenants that force the buyer to join the association, whether he likes it or not. Even when someone challenges the laws, he usually loses as the covenants are legally binding. It all starts with the builder because when a builder builds, he wants to make certain that the land value for the community stays high so that he can continue to sell his houses at a good price. The builder often starts off as the chairman of the homeowners association so that he can guide the formation of the rules and regulations. In one wealthy Florida community there are even regulations for local government and civil servants, including dress codes for policemen, taxi drivers, and mailmen. The only challenges that have gotten through the courts are those that show some regulation discriminates on the basis of race, religion, sex, or other characteristics of the homeowner.

Chapter 41

Unnecessary Words

41a. Conciseness

The following paragraph contains many words and phrases that are unnecessary. Rewrite the paragraph so that it is more concise.

It is definitely true that, as we all know, the topic of telling time is one that is of great importance to us all. This paragraph will discuss here the topic of time in our daily lives and how the concept of time has changed over time through the ages. Time plays an important role in people's lives because it is the essential measure against which other measurements of great and necessary importance were made. For example, we know that we can see that we measure the heart rates of our bodies in terms of time, and we know that we measure how fast our cars travel in terms of time. We organize our days and nights into whole segments of time, such as days, hours, minutes, and seconds, and from the very earliest beginnings of civilization people have counted the passage of time in terms of counting sunrises and sunsets or the movements of the moon as well as the movements of the sun in the sky overhead. For many centuries there was speculation about the nature of time that was mostly a philosophical discussion of how people perceive time and experience the passage of time. But in the twenty-first century science of today, since the work done by Albert Einstein, physicists have now come to realize that time is a definite dimension of the physical universe. Time is a measure of motion in space, not just some philosophical or theoretical thing that exists in people's minds as a concept they think about. The work of Albert Einstein, who was a physicist, also showed that time is not an absolute thing and that there is no such thing as a unique absolute time. It is known that people used to think that any event measured in time would be seen to take the same amount of time. To give an example of what this means, people used to think that two good clocks which are in good, accurate working order would agree on the time interval that it takes between two events. But history books tell us that the discovery that the speed of light appeared the same to every observer, no matter how he or she was moving, led to the theory of relativity. Now we know that time is seen by everyone relative to the observer who measures it. Each observer who observes time can have his or her own measure of time as recorded by the clock that he or she carries. Clocks that are carried by different observers do not necessarily have to agree. This view that observers do not have to agree on the time interval is a very different view of time from the older view of time that it is an absolute thing. However, as shown here, even with this notion that time is not an absolute

thing, we still in our lives today use time as a means of measurement.

41b. Clichés

Listed here are some word groups that many people regard as clichés. Try to think of a different way to express the same idea by writing a sentence using fresher language instead of the cliché.

1. white as snow

   _____

   _____

2. rain or shine

   _____

   _____

3. beat around the bush

   _____

   _____

4. easier said than done

   _____

   _____

5. big as a house

   _____

   _____

6. work your fingers to the bone

   _____

   _____

7. live happily ever after

_____

_____

8. first and foremost

_____

_____

9. to be turned on by

_____

_____

10. climb the ladder of success

_____

_____

41c. Pretentious Language

Listed here are some sentences that use what many people regard as pretentious language. Try to think of a different way to express the same idea by writing a sentence using plain English instead of the pretentious language. You may want to use a dictionary to determine the meaning of some words.

1. I unquestionably ascertained that the oration I planned to deliver to the assemblage of students required considerable revision.

_____

_____

2. I was rendered mute by the import of the situation.

_____

_____

3. Nathan is someone who is noted for his singularity.

_____

4. I shall slumber anon and awaken refreshed to meet the challenges of the pristine day.

   _____

   _____

5. The lucidity of the discourse was the source of significant veneration.

   _____

   _____

Chapter 42

Appropriate Words

42a–b: Standard English, Colloquialisms, Slang, and Regionalisms

Listed here are sentences that use some nonstandard words, colloquialisms, slang, and regionalisms. Try to find a different way to express the same idea by writing a sentence using standard words in place of the nonstandard and by using appropriate words in place of colloquialisms, slang, and regionalisms.

1. I ain't planning to take those kids to the circus.

   _____

   _____

2. Jason watched a sci-fi movie and then zonked out on the sofa.

   _____

   _____

3. Mark weren't planning to fight, but when Frank started to dis him, he decided he couldn't be a chicken.

   _____

   _____

4. I'm not uptight about the English exam, but I'm afraid I'm going to flunk the history exam.

   _____

   _____

5. Dad freaked out when he saw I had my tongue pierced.

   _____

   _____

42c. Levels of Formality

The following paragraph is written in a very informal tone. Revise it so that it is more formal and would be appropriate to print in a science news magazine intended for a general audience of reasonably well-educated readers.

Parents worried about their kids being grabbed by kidnappers have a new gimmick. Parents used to depend on taking photos with the old Polaroid or maybe getting a set of prints to stash in some computer file. But those methods aren't foolproof. Kids grow up and out of what they looked like in photos, and prints can be kind of hard to match. Now scientists bugged by not having a really foolproof way to nail a kid's identity have found a way that is looking good. Parents can get a sample of their baby's DNA material, which has great gobs of information about that particular kid. There's even a storage place set up for this in New Jersey. What's on file there, if someone wants it, is enough info to take a sample and match it against a hair, piece of skin, or even a couple of dots of blood. This is called DNA "fingerprinting," and it nails a kid's identity positively. What's really cool about this is that all the information from the genes stored at this place lasts as long as the person hangs around this planet—or longer. Grown-ups are pretty interested in getting themselves on file there too, especially those whose personal safety isn't high because of a dangerous job.

42d. Jargon and Technical Terms

Listed here are some sentences that use jargon and technical terms. Try to find a different way to express the same idea by writing a sentence using easily understandable language for a general audience. You may want to use a dictionary to find the meaning of unfamiliar words and terms.

1. My doctor told me that the antibiotic he prescribed for the inflammation of my gastrointestinal tract is counteracted by over-the-counter cold medications.

   _____

   _____

2. The learning facilitator of our pottery-making class doesn't receive enough monetary remuneration.

   _____

   _____

3. Our supervisor has asked that we revisit the problematic situation and provide input to its resolution.

   _____

   _____

4. Each candidate promised to implement no new revenue enhancements.

_____

_____

5. The scientist was studying the ferromagnetic properties of various Paleolithic artifacts.

_____

_____

42e. General and Specific Words

The following paragraph contains some general terms that are underlined which need to be replaced by more specific terms. The paragraph also contains some specific terms that are underlined which need to be replaced by more general terms. Revise the paragraph by replacing these terms with more appropriate ones.

People like driving up for fast food, and now so do their <u>animals</u>. A new fast-food industry has begun for drive-in dog food, and the menu is entirely for <u>spaniels and collies</u>. These new <u>things</u> offer treats to dogs with dog biscuits shaped to resemble <u>food.</u> The dog biscuits are made from foods that help keep dogs healthy. The biscuits are <u>flavored</u> so that dogs don't get tired of the same thing. Customers love the idea of <u>driving their trucks to</u> a doggy drive-in after picking up their own <u>stuff.</u> So far the menu has been limited to dog biscuits, but <u>some men</u> will come up with new ideas for better <u>bone-shaped biscuits</u> for dogs.

42f. Concrete and Abstract Words

The following paragraph contains some abstract words that are underlined. Change those abstract terms to more concrete ones.

When hikers reach a stream, they often decide to cross where the <u>route approaches</u> the water. But this may not be the best place at which to cross. Water usually moves most swiftly at the narrowest part of the stream. So, hikers should instead look for another spot where the stream widens. Here the current often <u>has less velocity</u> and may be easier to walk through. When hikers are carrying a backpack, they should loosen the shoulder straps and hip belt before <u>immersion</u> so that they can toss off the pack <u>if difficulties occur.</u> Some hikers find that if they suddenly hit a depression in the streambed, the weight of the backpack can toss them off balance. Another aid to crossing a stream is a good hiking stick. It can serve as another leg, offering better balance when there are <u>dangerous elements present.</u> It is helpful to remove unneeded <u>clothing</u> before crossing a stream with a swift current because the water can drag against <u>wet outerwear.</u> The hiker should also take each step slowly and deliberately. The forward foot should be planted firmly before the rear foot is moved. Finally, the careful hiker never hurries across a stream.

42g. Denotation and Connotation

Each of the following words has either a positive or negative connotation. Think of an alternative term that has the opposite connotation.

EXAMPLE

devoted   obsessed
_____

1. notorious   _____

2. assertive   _____

3. right-wing   _____

4. orderly, well organized   _____

5. garbage collector   _____

6. pre-owned   _____

7. dirt   _____

8. fragrance   _____

9. economical   _____

10. big spender   _____

Some connotations are personal and not always shared by others. If you have connotations for any of these terms, write them here.

1. lake _____

2. ice _____

3. summer _____

4. chemistry _____

5. automobile _____

PART SEVEN
ESL CONCERNS

Chapter 43

American Style in Writing

If your first language is not English, write a paragraph describing how the writing style in your native language differs from the American style in writing. Issues you might consider in your paragraph include conciseness, topic announcement, organization, and source citation. If your first language is English, interview someone whose native language is something other than English, and write a paragraph describing how that person's writing style differs from the American style.

_____

_____

_____

_____

_____

_____

_____

_____

_____

Chapter 44

Verbs

The following paragraph contains some errors in the verbs. Underline the errors and write your corrections above the words you underlined.

When people from other countries will shop in American supermarkets, they find an amazing supply of items other than grocery items. On one aisle, a shopper will discovered, for example, toiletry items such as toothbrushes, toothpaste, deodorant, and shampoo. On another aisle be paper towels, garbage bags, and cleaning supplies. Sometimes the choices would be confusing. But the choices do not ended with the shopping itself. Even when the shopping have conclude, the shopper may have decisions to make. For example, the person behind the checkout counter may asked if the customer would want the purchases in a plastic bag or a paper bag. Of course, if Americans was to shop in stores and bazaars in other countries, they can find the process just as confusing.

In the following paragraph underline the correct form of the verb that is needed.

In the United States, students hope (to learn, learning) more than just the subject matter they are studying. They

believe that if they (study, will study) a subject thoroughly, ask questions, and even (disagree, will disagree) with

certain opinions of writers and scholars, they (will become, become) better thinkers as well. Students from other

countries may find it difficult at first to practice critical-thinking skills in American classrooms because (to question,

questioning) an authority or the written word may be a sign of disrespect in their country. Another problem that

students from other countries may encounter in American classrooms involves writing assignments. Whereas

American students are comfortable with (choosing, to choose) topics for writing that argue accepted ideas, students

from other countries may have difficulty (to express, expressing) their opinions without (apologizing, to apologize) for

them because (discussing, to discuss) controversial topics may be considered rude in their country. Obviously,

students' cultural backgrounds affect many aspects of college life, including how they approach the educational

experience.

Use the following verb forms in sentences of your own. If the second word can be separated from the verb in your sentence, a pronoun is included in parentheses.

1. should + verb

   _____

   _____

2. will be + verb

_____

_____

3. may + verb

_____

_____

4. can + verb

_____

_____

5. do + verb

_____

_____

6. may have been + verb

_____

_____

7. fall behind

_____

_____

8. get out of

_____

_____

9. look like

_____

_____

10. run across

11. tear (it) down

12. call (it) off

13. call (her) up

14. try (it) out

Chapter 45

Omitted Words

In the following paragraph there are omitted verbs and subjects. Revise the paragraph to conform to standard English by inserting verbs and subjects where they are needed.

When importing ivory became illegal in the United States in 1989, engineers and material scientists searched for substitutes for natural ivory. For piano makers, the ban on ivory brought on the problem of how to make piano keys after the supply on hand used up. While conservationists and elephant lovers want people stop using ivory, many pianists who have tested plastic substitutes about to abandon hope of having new pianos with satisfactory substitutes. However, may be a solution. A team of experts has produced a substitute that may satisfy many piano builders and piano players. This new synthetic ivory both resembles natural ivory and has a similar microscopic structure. But even with a substitute for piano keys now available, the market for ivory not decrease as piano makers never been major consumers of ivory. The largest consumers of ivory in the world are Asian manufacturers of signature stamps, but even have given up their use of ivory and switching to substitutes.

Chapter 46

Repeated Words

In the following sentences, underline the unnecessary words that repeat the subject, pronoun, or adverb.

1. Students in my class they are looking forward to the upcoming vacation.

2. The book that I wanted to read it was not in the library.

3. My teacher found the book that I left it in the classroom.

4. The apartment building where I live there has two swimming pools.

5. The child returned the dog that I had lost it.

6. The pie in the refrigerator it is for tonight's party.

7. The book drop where library books are placed there is full.

8. My aunt called on the new cellular telephone that she had it installed in her car.

Complete the following sentences being careful not to repeat the subject as a pronoun before the verb and being careful not to add unnecessary words when relative pronouns and relative adverbs introduce clauses.

1. Children in my family

_____

_____

2. The computer that I want to buy

_____

_____

3. The cat sat on the blanket that I left

_____

_____

4. The car that I drive

   _____

   _____

5. The girl who wants to borrow my notes

   _____

   _____

Chapter 47

Count and Noncount Nouns

The following paragraph has both count and noncount nouns. Choose the correct form in parentheses and underline it.

In American supermarkets, new (products, product) and (produce, produces) are constantly being added to the shelves. Children are attracted to new snack foods, and adults are frequently tempted to buy items with (information, informations) about health benefits. To increase consumer (confidence, confidences) in package labeling, the Food and Drug Administration has announced new (guideline, guidelines) for various claims food manufacturers add to their labels. Products that are advertised as "low (fat, fats)" have to provide (evidence, evidences) on the label and meet new government (standard, standards). For items that appeal to children, the amount of (sugar, sugars) must be clearly indicated. Particularly helpful are the new regulations on serving size because consumers in America have become very conscious of the amount of (protein, proteins) and (fat, fats) that they eat as well as the number of (calorie, calories).

Write a sentence for each of the words listed below. Some are count nouns, some are noncount nouns, and some have both a count meaning and a noncount meaning.

1. research

    _____

    _____

2. difficulty (as a count noun) and difficulty (as a noncount noun)

    _____

    _____

3. table

    _____

    _____

4. computer

    _____

5. light (as a count noun) and light (as a noncount noun)

_____

_____

6. truth

_____

_____

Chapter 48

Adjectives and Adverbs

48a–b. Placement and Order

Reorder the following word clusters to create correct sentences, being careful about the placement of the adjectives, adverbs, and nouns. Don't add any words, and be sure to capitalize the first letter of the first word in your sentence.

1. new   eager   three   students   entered   quickly   the   classroom

   _____

   _____

2. Japanese   favorite   food   her   is   sushi

   _____

   _____

3. girls   the   young   were   frightened   easily

   _____

   _____

4. sometimes   experience   I   homesickness   intense

   _____

   _____

5. almost   forget   never   I   anniversary   our

   _____

   _____

Write a paragraph of your own correctly using at least three adjectives and three adverbs. You may want to write about learning to speak a second language.

   _____

   _____

_____

_____

_____

_____

_____

_____

_____

48c–d. A/An/The, Some/Any, Much/Many, Little/Few, Less/Fewer, Enough, No

In the paragraph below, underline the correct word in parentheses.

In northern India there is (a, an) conflict between wildlife officials and Gujjar herders of water buffalo. (A, An, The) Indian government wants to turn the area into a national park, to be called the Fajaji National Park, but for the last ten years, local water buffalo herders refuse to move off the land. The Gujjars keep herding their water buffalo, despite warnings that the animals are eating up too (much, many) of the vegetation and that soon there will be (less, few) areas that have not been destroyed by the herding. Several decades ago, the Gujjars agreed to migrate every summer to give the forests a chance to grow again, but communities in the areas they migrated to refused to accept the Gujjars because they needed (a, an, the) land for their own grazing, and they didn't have (fewer, enough, no) land to share. As a result, the Gujjars now stay in the forest throughout (a, an, the) year. Government officials keep on warning of (a, an, the) dangers of erosion in the forests where Gujjar herding has stripped the land. While (some, any, much) environmental groups say that these forest dwellers have as much right to the land as the animals, other groups support the government's attempt to move the Gujjars. The continued grazing by water buffalos risks using up the (few, less, little) food sources of elephants and other animals. Government officials plan to make (a, an) offer to the Gujjars to move them to settlements on the edge of the forests and to have them feed their animals in stalls. Park officials want to find (a, an) solution soon because they say that both the park and the Gujjars will suffer if the present situation continues.

Write a paragraph of your own correctly using each of the following words at least once: a, an, the, some, any, many, few, less, enough. You may want to write about how two countries vary in their concerns about wildlife.

Chapter 49

Prepositions

Write sentences of your own in which you use the following prepositions.

1. on (as a preposition of time)

   _____

   _____

2. on (as a preposition of place)

   _____

   _____

3. at (as a preposition of time)

   _____

   _____

4. at (as a preposition of place)

   _____

   _____

5. in (as a preposition of time)

   _____

   _____

6. in (as a preposition of place)

   _____

   _____

7. of (to show a relationship between a part and the whole)

   _____

   _____

8. of (to show content)

_____

_____

9. for (to show purpose)

_____

_____

Chapter 50

Idioms

Write sentences of your own in which you use the following idioms.

1. the old college try

   _____

   _____

2. took off

   _____

   _____

3. on the ball

   _____

   _____

4. live high on the hog

   _____

   _____

5. help out

   _____

   _____

6. the bottom line

   _____

   _____

7. come across

   _____

   _____

8. look into (meaning to study or check on something)

_____

_____

9. show up

_____

_____

10. fall behind

_____

_____

PART EIGHT
RESEARCH

Chapter 51

Finding a Topic

For each of the research paper general subjects listed below, narrow the subject into a manageable topic for a research paper which would be due two weeks from the date of the assignment. Then formulate a research question about your topic, and formulate a thesis statement that answers your research question.

EXAMPLE

Subject: World War II

Topic: How WWII brought more women into the workforce

Research Question: How did the economic demands of World War II affect women's roles in the American workforce?

Thesis Statement: Because World War II created an historic demand for manufacturing while simultaneously removing almost one-half of the men of working age, women entered the workforce to take up the slack, forever changing societal ideals of "women's work."

1. Subject:Sports

Topic:

_____

_____

Research Question:

_____

_____

Thesis Statement:

_____

2. Subject: Computers

   Topic:

   _____

   _____

   Research Question:

   _____

   _____

   Thesis Statement:

   _____

   _____

3. Subject: Cultural Differences

   Topic:

   _____

   _____

   Research Question:

   _____

   _____

   Thesis Statement:

   _____

   _____

4. Subject: Cloning

   Topic:

   _____

Research Question:

_____

_____

Thesis Statement:

_____

_____

5. Subject: The Media and Politics

   Topic:

   _____

   _____

   Research Question:

   _____

   _____

   Thesis Statement:

   _____

   _____

Chapter 52

Searching for Information

Using the following source information, prepare a bibliographic entry on the card provided here.

An article by Frederick Meisnier entitled "Historical Migrations of Foods," in the May 1993 issue of International Cuisine, pages 18–27.

Identify each of the research sources listed below as a primary or secondary source for a research paper about Ernest Hemingway.

EXAMPLE

"Hills Like White Elephants" (a short story by Hemingway)   <u>primary</u>

1. <u>The Hemingway Women</u> (a book about Hemingway)   _____

2. <u>The Sun Also Rises</u> (a novel by Hemingway)   _____

3. an encyclopedia article about Hemingway   _____

4. an informative television program about Hemingway   _____

5. <u>Hemingway on the Spanish Civil War</u> (a book of letters written by Hemingway and compiled by an editor)   _____

6. an Internet site about Hemingway maintained by *The New York Times*   _____

Chapter 53

Evaluating Sources

Look at the citation in the next exercise (Chapter 46), and evaluate it for use in an informative paper on world spices.

Your evaluation based on the bibliographic citation (author, timeliness, publisher/producer, audience)

_____

_____

_____

_____

_____

Your evaluation based on the content (accuracy, comprehensiveness, credibility, fairness, objectivity, relevance, timeliness)

_____

_____

_____

_____

_____

Chapter 54

Taking Notes

Write a summary and also a paraphrase of the following paragraph. Assume that you read the paragraph as part of an article by Frederick Meisnier entitled "Historical Migrations of Foods," in the May 1993 issue of *International Cuisine*, pages 18–27.

"One of the world's most widely used spices is the chili pepper. It gives the characteristic fire to one of India's most well-known foods, curry. In Hungary, chili pepper appears as paprika, adding a crucial bite to the flavor of goulash, and in Italy the use of chili peppers in pepperoni makes the spice a common ingredient in Italian food. The hot flavor of chilies became a staple in various foods of China, Thailand, and other Oriental countries. Five hundred years ago, however, no one in these countries had heard of the chili pepper or even had a word for it, for it was one of the treasures brought back from the New World by Christopher Columbus. When Columbus returned with his new spice, its use soon spread around the globe because it was an interesting addition to the world's spice cabinets and because it traveled well in dried form. There is even evidence of chili peppers being used as a condiment in China within a few decades after it appeared on Spanish tables. The most likely route to the Orient was by sea as the Portuguese engaged in active trading with China, particularly after the founding of their trade colony in Macao. While the Spanish were the first Europeans to encounter the New World peppers, the pepper did not become a distinctive spice in Spanish cooking. It was looked upon more as a curiosity or ornamental than as a fiery way to liven up food. Now, after centuries of use in Central and South America, the chili pepper is finally becoming more popular in North American markets through the increasing interest in Indian, Indonesian, Thai, Vietnamese, and other non-European cuisines."

Your summary:

_____

_____

_____

_____

_____

_____

_____

_____

Your paraphrase:

_____

_____

_____

_____

_____

_____

_____

_____

_____

Chapter 55

Using Sources

Write an informative paragraph on chili peppers by using the information in the exercise in Chapter 46 as well as information from two other sources you have found through research. Incorporate information using paraphrasing, summarizing, and quoting as appropriate from all three sources by using parenthetical citations in MLA format. List the three sources at the end of your paragraph using MLA format for references. (Refer to Chapter 52 for information on parenthetical citations and references.)

PART NINE
ONLINE

Chapters 56, 57, 58, 59

Research Online, Web Resources, Evaluating Internet Sources, and Citing Internet Sources

Conduct online research on one of the following American writers: William Faulkner, Willa Cather, or Toni Morrison. List three credible Internet sources for information on the writer you have researched using MLA online citation form.

Source

_____

_____

_____

Source

_____

_____

_____

Source

_____

_____

_____

Conduct online research on one of the following topics: the juvenile justice system in the United States, the use of music therapy to treat psychological disorders, or the history of NATO. List three credible Internet sources for information on the topic you have researched using APA online citation form.

Source

_____

_____

_____

Source _____

_____

_____

_____

Source _____

_____

_____

_____

PART TEN

DOCUMENTATION

Chapter 60

Documenting in MLA Style

Included here is a paragraph about women hikers. Following the paragraph are some sentences with information that can be added to the paragraph either as direct quotations or as information whose source must be cited. Rewrite the paragraph so that you add at least two direct quotations and one parenthetical reference to a source whose information you also use but in your own words. Be sure to integrate the quotations into the paragraph, cite the sources in the paragraph, and include a list of Works Cited (in MLA format) at the end of the paragraph.

Among the other worlds of outdoor sports and recreation that women were entering before the turn of the century was hiking. Annie Smith Peck joined the list of great alpinists when she reached the peak of the Matterhorn in 1895. She was the first woman to wear pants for climbing, even though at that time women all wore floor-length skirts. Peck continued her climbing and hiking until she was seventy-five years old, including the historic first ascent of Mount Huascaran in Peru, a climb that went above 22,000 feet. In 1901, six years after Peck's assault on the Matterhorn, women joined the first Sierra Club hike. Despite Peck's famous knickerbocker pants, the Sierra Club's stated policy was that women wear skirts which could be no shorter than halfway from knee to ankle. Female hikers in great climbs became increasingly common, though not always as colorful as the famous Grandma Gatewood (Emma Gatewood), the first woman to hike the entire Appalachian Trail in one continuous stretch, in 1955. At the age of sixty-seven she hiked in sneakers and slept on a plastic shower curtain. Grandma Gatewood went on to hike the great Appalachian Trail two more times in her career.

Material to add to your version of the paragraph:

1. The historian Iris Koach, in a book entitled *Women in Sports* (published in New York in 1992 by Littleton and Crane Publishing Company), wrote the following sentence which appears on page 81:

149

"Annie Smith Peck, a product of genteel Victorian wealth and exclusive private schooling, became intrigued with the idea of laying aside her scholarly efforts in order to scale the Matterhorn."

On page 172, Koach mentions Emma Gatewood:

"With little publicity and less interest in commercial support for her efforts, Emma Gatewood continued to set hiking records until well into her eighties. She was an inspiration for women who saw themselves as too frail or inexperienced to hike on their own or without the support of a group of men."

2. The following sentence appears on page 45 of *Hiking American Trails* by William Byler (published in 1990 by Middlebauer Press in New York):

"By the 1950's, equipment for hiking filled specialty catalogs and took over more and more space in sporting goods stores. The selection of hiking boots, tents, backpacks, cooking utensils, and other gear had become a complicated science."

Your version of the original paragraph with the material added:

_____

_____

_____

_____

_____

_____

_____

_____

_____

_____

_____

_____

_____

_____

_____

_____

_____

_____

_____

Your Works Cited page for your version of the paragraph you wrote in the last exercise:

_____

_____

_____

_____

_____

_____

_____

_____

_____

_____

_____

_____

_____

_____

_____

Listed here are a variety of sources which were used to write a paper. Using every entry listed, prepare a Works Cited page according to MLA style.

1. A book by Martin Joos entitled *The Five Clocks* published in New York by Harcourt, Brace, and World in 1962. The paper cited information from pages 12 and 22 of this book.

2. A book by Stephen Duggan and Betty Drury entitled The Rescue of Science and Learning published in New York by Macmillan in 1948. The paper cited information from pages 63–62.

3. A book entitled *Writing Centers in Context:Twelve Case Studies*, edited by Joyce A. Kinkead and Jeanette Harris and published in Urbana, Illinois, by NCTE in 1993. The paper cited information from page 74.

4. A poem entitled "Night Shadows" appearing in an anthology entitled *The New Gothic*, compiled and edited by Marvin Greenwood and published in New York by Chaosium in 1998. The paper cited information form page 66.

5. A magazine article by Robert Lillo entitled "The Electronic Industry Braces for Hard Times" appearing on pages 18–23 of the February 14, 1996 edition of *Business Weekly* magazine.

6. An interview with Nina Totenberg on the television program *Nightline*, produced by ABC and aired on channel WILI out of Chicago on November 23, 1995.

7. A citation from William Shakespeare's Hamlet taken from a collection of Shakespeare's work on CD-ROM published by CMCReSearch in 1989. The CD-ROM program does not list a place of publication.

8. Material from an online information service, Dialog, from file 102, item 0346142. The material came from an article by Walter S. Baer entitled "Telecommunications Technology in the 1990s," published in the June 1994 edition of *Computer Science* magazine. The article began on page 152 and continued on various pages throughout the magazine.

Your Works Cited page for the sources listed in this exercise:

Chapter 61

Documenting in APA Style

Included here is the same paragraph about women hikers as used in the first exercise for Chapter 60. Following the paragraph are some sentences with information that can be added to the paragraph either as direct quotations or as information whose source must be cited. Rewrite the paragraph so that you add at least two direct quotations and one parenthetical reference to a source whose information you also use but in your own words. Be sure to integrate the quotations into the paragraph, cite the sources in the paragraph, and include a list of the works you cited (in APA format) at the end of the paragraph.

Among the other worlds of outdoor sports and recreation that women were entering before the turn of the century was hiking. Annie Smith Peck joined the list of great alpinists when she reached the peak of the Matterhorn in 1895. She was the first woman to wear pants for climbing, even though at that time women all wore floor-length skirts. Peck continued her climbing and hiking until she was seventy-five years old, including the historic first ascent of Mount Huascaran in Peru, a climb that went above 22,000 feet. In 1901, six years after Peck's assault on the Matterhorn, women joined the first Sierra Club hike. Despite Peck's famous knickerbocker pants, the Sierra Club's stated policy was that women wear skirts which could be no shorter than halfway from knee to ankle. Female hikers in great climbs became increasingly common, though not always as colorful as the famous Grandma Gatewood (Emma Gatewood), the first woman to hike the entire Appalachian Trail in one continuous stretch, in 1955. At the age of sixty-seven she hiked in sneakers and slept on a plastic shower curtain. Grandma Gatewood went on to hike the great Appalachian Trail two more times in her career.

Material to add to your version of the paragraph:

1. The historian Iris Koach, in a book entitled *Women in Sports* (published in New York in 1992 by Littleton and Crane Publishing Company), wrote the following sentence which appears on page 81:

"Annie Smith Peck, a product of genteel Victorian wealth and exclusive private schooling, became intrigued with the idea of laying aside her scholarly efforts in order to scale the Matterhorn."

On page 172, Koach mentions Emma Gatewood:

"With little publicity and less interest in commercial support for her efforts, Emma Gatewood continued to set hiking records until well into her eighties. She was an inspiration for women who saw themselves as too frail or inexperienced to hike on their own or without the support of a group of men."

2. The following sentence appears on page 45 of *Hiking American Trails* by William Byler (published in 1990 by Middlebauer Press in New York):

"By the 1950's, equipment for hiking filled specialty catalogs and took over more and more space in sporting goods stores. The selection of hiking boots, tents, backpacks, cooking utensils, and other gear had become a complicated science."

Your version of the original paragraph with the material added:

_____

_____

_____

_____

_____

_____

_____

_____

_____

_____

_____

_____

_____

_____

_____

_____

_____

_____

Your References page for your version of the paragraph you wrote in the last exercise:

_____

_____

_____

_____

_____

_____

_____

_____

_____

_____

_____

_____

_____

_____

_____

_____

Listed here are a variety of sources which were used to write a paper. Using every entry listed, prepare a Reference page according to APA style.

1. A book by Martin Joos entitled *The Five Clocks* published in New York by Harcourt, Brace, and World in 1962. The paper cited information from pages 12 and 22 of this book.

2. A book by Stephen Duggan and Betty Drury entitled *The Rescue of Science and Learning* published in New York by Macmillan in 1948. The paper cited information from pages 63–62.

3. A book entitled *Writing Centers in Context: Twelve Case Studies*, edited by Joyce A. Kinkead and Jeanette Harris and published in Urbana, Illinois, by NCTE in 1993. The paper cited information from page 74.

4. A work entitled "Vengeance" appearing in the anthology entitled Poetry in the Modern Age, compiled and edited by Jason Metier and published in San Francisco by New Horizons in 1994. The paper cited information from page 54.

5. A magazine article by Robert Lillo entitled "The Electronic Industry Braces for Hard Times" appearing on pages 18–23 of the February 14, 1996 edition of *Business Weekly* magazine.

6. An interview with Nina Totenberg on the television program *Nightline*, produced by ABC and aired on channel WILI out of Chicago on November 23, 1995.

7. A citation from William Shakespeare's *Hamlet* taken from a collection of Shakespeare's work on CD-ROM published by CMCReSearch in 1989. The CD-ROM program does not list a place of publication.

8. Material from an online information service, Dialog, from file 102, item 0346142. The material came from an article by Walter S. Baer entitled "Telecommunications Technology in the 1990s," published in the June 1994 edition of *Computer Science* magazine. The article began on page 152 and continued on various pages throughout the magazine.

Your Reference page for the sources listed in this exercise:

_____

_____

_____

_____

_____

_____

_____

_____

Chapter 62

Documenting in Other Styles

Choose the letter for the preferred documentation style for source citations on the topics.

Topics   Source Citations

1. War-time journalism   _____   A. Chicago Manual of Style

2. Astronomical calculations   _____   B. CBE

3. Journal of American History   _____   C. The Associated Press Style Book and Libel Manual

4. Biological control   _____   D. The AMS Author Handbook
   of garden pests

5. Geometrical theories   _____   E. AIP Style Manual

Chapter 63

Document Design

63a. Placement and Order

Group the information in the paragraph below into a list that will be less crowded and have more white space.

The restaurant guide has lists of ethnic restaurants. They list Chinese restaurants in the city. They also list Italian restaurants and Mexican restaurants. As an extra feature, they list ethnic restaurants by neighborhood.

63b. Visual Elements

1. Put the information in the paragraph below into a bar graph to add interest to your Web page.

College freshmen at the university took an average of 18 credit hours per semester. Sophomores took an average of 16 hours per semester and junior and seniors took an average of 12 hours per semester.

2. Now put the same information in a line graph.

63c. Web Page Design

Draw a visual plan for an online clothing store that would include the following pages:

- Home Page

- Men's clothing

- Women's clothing

- Children's clothing

- Dresses

- Women's shoes

- Toddlers

- Children's sizes 5-10

63d. Paper Preparation

Identify each of the pages below as belonging in MLA or APA.

1. Title Page   _____

2. First page, with author information   _____

3. Tables (on a separate page)   _____

4. Footnotes   _____

5. Works Cited List   _____

6. Appendixes   _____

7. End notes   _____

Chapter 64

Public Writing

64a. Business Letters

Write a letter recommending a person for employment. The body of your text should contain at least two paragraphs. The person to whom you are writing is Phil Brannan, New Projects Director. The address is 128 Cedar Ave., Overland Park, Kansas 66212. Be sure to send a copy to Monica Oden, Director of Human Resources.

64b. Resume Styles

Take the following Skills Resume and reorganize it into a Reverse Chronological Resume.

Donald Bryant

3256 Winslow Lane
Springfield, MO 65802
(417) 555-5300
dbryant@dotcom.net

PROFESSIONAL OBJECTIVE

A career in hotel management that would involve guest relations, scheduling and vendor management.

EDUCATION

Johnson County Community College
Associate in Applied Science Degree in Hotel/Motel Management
GPA (4.0 scale): 3.6
Major-Related Courses:
> HOSPITALITY MANAGEMENT FUNDAMENTALS, FOOD MANAGEMENT, SUPERVISORY MANAGEMENT, HOSPITALITY LAW, SEMINAR IN HOUSEKEEPING OPERATIONS, HOTEL SALES AND MARKETING, ADVANCED HOSPITALITY MANAGEMENT, FRONT OFFICE MANAGEMENT, HOTEL ACCOUNTING

SKILLS

Accounting
- Student Senate Treasurer
- Did bookkeeping for local hobby store

Scheduling
- Events coordinator for Student Senate
- Scheduled work hours for College book store employees

Vendor relations
- Worked with various food vendors at mall food court

WORK EXPERIENCE

Assistant Manager, Oak Park Mall Food Court; August 2001 to present
Assistant Manager, College Bookstore; Fall 2000-Spring 2001

Chapter 65

Writing About Literature

65a. Ways to Write About Literature

Read a play or short story. Briefly describe each of the following aspects of the work:

1. Plot – How do events connect? Do some events foreshadow others?

   _____

   _____

   _____

   _____

   _____

2. Characters – Who is the main character in the work? Does this character change and if so, how?

   _____

   _____

   _____

   _____

   _____

3. Narrative Structure – Do the events proceed in chronological order? What clues does the author provide?

   _____

   _____

   _____

   _____

   _____

4. Narrator – Is a character telling the story? If so, how does this affect how we see the action? If not, how much are we shown (thoughts, movement in place, time, etc.)?

_____

_____

_____

_____

_____

5. Gender – How does the work portray men and women?   Is there a difference in how each is portrayed?

_____

_____

_____

_____

_____

6. Genre - How would you describe the type of literature this work represents (give specific reasons for your choice)?

_____

_____

_____

_____

_____

65c. Literary Terms

Define each of the following:

1. Genre _____

2. Imagery _____

3. Metaphor _____

4. Plot _____

5. Setting _____

6. Symbol _____

7. Theme _____

65d. Conventions in Writing About Literature

Next to each example below, identify the verb tense that should be used.

1. A biography of the author _____

2. A brief summary of a short story _____

3. Introducing a line from a poem _____

4. Describing the environment in which a novel was written _____

ANSWER KEY

In some cases, responses to exercises will vary, in particular when original sentences and paragraphs are to be written in response to the exercises. Other exercises require specific revision, but the method of revision may vary. In those cases, one example of a possible revision is provided in this Answer Key. Other exercises can only be revised or responded to in one specific way, and in those cases, the answers are provided here.

Part One

Chapter 3
Paragraphs

3a. Unity

Responses will vary but should mention that the sentence about the weather in Tibet should be deleted for the sake of unity.

3b. Coherence

Responses will vary but should mention that although the paragraph is well written, it would benefit from added transition between sentences.

3c. Development

Responses will vary but should mention that the paragraph lacks adequate development.

Part Two

Chapter 6
Comma Splices and Fused Sentences

Responses will vary, but one possible revision is provided here.

Our country seems to be going through a change in attitudes. Unlike our forefathers, we Americans are now encouraged to get as much as possible as quickly as possible. This attitude is expressed on television; advertising also plays on this appeal. Many see a relationship between these current attitudes and gambling on lotteries. It is easy to understand why more and more people are handing their money over to chance, fate, and luck if what they are looking for is instant gratification. Statistics show this attitude is growing: in the late 80s, state lotteries grew an average of 17.5 percent annually—roughly as fast as the computer industry. High-tech advertising for the lotteries takes attention away from the fact that a player has virtually no chance of winning. Advertisements focus instead on the fantasy of what it would be like to win. Surveys conducted by state lotteries show that few players have a clear understanding of how dismal their odds of winning really are. A player has a better chance of being struck by lightening than of winning a lottery.

Chapter 7
Subject-Verb Agreement

is

weighs

finds

sell

is

want

depends

is

strike

do

are

are

is

Sentences will vary but the verb forms should be as follows:

1. Singular

2. Plural

3. Plural

4. Plural

5. Plural

6. Plural

7. Singular

8. Singular

9. Singular

10. Plural

11. Singular

12. Singular or plural depending upon how committee is used

13. Singular

14. Plural

15. Singular

16. Singular

17. Plural

18. Singular

19. Plural

20. Singular

21. Plural

22. Singular

23. Plural

Chapter 8
Sentence Fragments

1. complete sentence

2. complete sentence

3. fragment

4. complete sentence

5. fragment

6. complete sentence

7. fragment

8. complete sentence

9. fragment

10. fragment

11. fragment

12. complete sentence

Chapter 9
Dangling and Misplaced Modifiers

9a. Dangling Modifiers

The great memorials in the nation's capital are slowly deteriorating. Having faced the elements for seven decades, even casual tourists can see that the Lincoln Memorial is wearing down. Water is causing the steel structures embedded in the concrete slabs to deteriorate. At the Jefferson Memorial, which is built on clay fill, the steps are starting to pull away from the base of the monument, and there are cracks appearing in the dome. Being washed daily, details in the marble carvings of both monuments are falling off. Air pollution and acid rain are also contributing to the gradual disintegration. To find a solution, constant studies by the National Park Service are being conducted, but the caretakers of the monuments are pessimistic. Exposure to the elements, they say, causes some deterioration that cannot be stopped. Looking more like ruins than buildings, it is hard to watch these noble monuments wear away.

9b. Misplaced Modifiers

The Food and Drug Administration (FDA) claims in a report issued recently that it has found tiny amounts of drug residue in milk samples. The level of contamination is so low that there is no real safety problem in the nation's milk supply, but a ban has been put on one drug, sulfamethazine, found in a few samples, to prohibit its use by farmers with beef cattle and pigs. The FDA has already banned the use of sulfamethazine with milk cows. However, among members of Congress, there is still concern that some dairy farmers or veterinarians use the drug improperly even though recent testing of a large number of milk samples found only a few traces of sulfa drugs. The FDA is now calling on dairy farmers and veterinarians to eliminate all illegal uses of veterinary drug products. <u>Almost all</u> farmers are already complying with this order.

9c. Additional Modifier Exercises

Responses will vary, but possible revisions are provided here.

1. Scientists have discovered Cro-Magnon man was human because he used primitive tools.
2. Using a large flashlight, Bob stunned the pit bull.
3. As we walked into the house's entryway, the lamp glowed warmly.
4. Mark on the enclosed card which magazine you choose.
5. Sue found a woman's emerald bracelet.
6. As one approaches the city from the west, the sports arena is quite a sight.

Chapter 10
Parallel Constructions

Recently, two pilots, <u>one in a 175-seat commercial airliner</u> and <u>the other one in a small, twin-engine corporate jet</u>, were barreling toward each other. On the instrument panel of the commercial jet, <u>a small air traffic screen flashed a yellow circle</u> and <u>a voice announced, "Traffic."</u> As the yellow circle approached the center of the screen, it changed to a red square. The voice said loudly, "Climb, climb."<u>As he noticed the red square</u> and <u>as he pulled up</u>, the pilot saw the other craft fly past several hundred feet below. The voice that called out the warning was <u>not the copilot</u> but <u>the latest audiovisual aid to arrive in cockpits of planes</u>, a traffic alert and collision avoidance system. The Federal Aviation Administration has issued an order <u>that this system must be installed in 20 percent of all large commercial planes by next year</u> and <u>that this system must be installed in 20 percent of all large commercial planes using American airspace within the next three years</u>. The system works by <u>computing the distance between planes</u>, <u>warning planes when they get within six miles of each other</u>, and then deciding which plane should climb and which should descend to avoid a collision.

Chapter 11
Consistency/Avoiding Shifts

Responses will vary, but one possible revision is provided here.

High school proms used to be dances where students dressed up in suits and dresses and celebrated their coming graduation, but now they have to spend a lot of money for a tuxedo or elegant formal dress. Proms have become big business as formalwear shops and limousine services offer their services in advertising campaigns. Tuxedo rental shops across the country report that proms, not weddings, account for the major proportion of their business. The typical expenses now include the tuxedo rental, prom tickets, corsage, dinner, and limousine rental. High-school graduates can easily spend $300 on the dance, and that may be just for the basics. Prom-goers can spend additional funds for the latest fashions in tuxes, and they can buy photos for $50 or more. Even when the prom is over, there are other expenses. Some graduates go away for the whole weekend, often to a resort hotel. So there are additional costs for a hotel, and if parents are along as chaperones, it is necessary to add in the cost of their rooms and meals too. High-school graduates insist that this is all necessary as a rite of passage, but parents who often have to contribute at least part of the funds do not appreciate the expense.

Chapter 12
Faulty Predication

With the present concern for the environment, some companies are trying to increase their sales by advertising their products as environmentally safe. The makers of some plastic trash bags, for example, are claiming that their plastic is degradable. The reason for the claim is that there are additives that cause the product to break down after prolonged exposure to sunlight. Biodegradability, they assert, occurs when there is photodegradability, a breakdown by sunlight. But since most trash bags are buried in landfills, the benefits of photodegradability are questionable. Thus, the government has stated that one way to improve deceptive advertising claims is to eliminate false or misleading information.

Chapter 13
Coordination and Subordination

Responses will vary, but one possible revision is provided here.

Americans have become videotape addicts. Because over 75 percent of all American households now have videocassette recorders, hotels hope to make their guests feel at home by providing equipment for watching videotapes. Some of the largest hotel chains in the country have added videocassette recorders in the rooms which can be used by renting videocassettes from shops in the hotel. In these shops, which have a good selection of recent movies for guests to view in their rooms, hotels guests can show their room key and can rent a movie at a reasonable rate. Other hotels don't want to bother with stores in the lobby, and they are exploring a different option. They are adding automated video dispensing machines in their lobbies that hold hundreds of titles and have new releases as well as standard favorites. One hotel chain, which has a lot of large business conventions, has investigated another approach. It is offering to distribute to guests videotapes that the corporation holding the convention wants its participants to see. Corporations like this because the videotapes can convey some of the key ideas being presented at the convention. Videotape players in hotel rooms may soon be standard equipment, just as television sets were added years ago. When Americans became addicted to television, they expected to watch television in their hotel rooms.

Chapter 14
Sentence Clarity

Responses will vary, but one possible revision is provided here.

A new approach to using computers may be to jot handwritten notes onto an electronic pad. This is done by a special pen that projects a narrow light beam onto the pad. For computer users who have had to rely on entering data into a computer by means of a keyboard, it is a major step forward in using computers. Typing is more distracting than writing for many people who are not skilled typists but who use computers frequently. For the last twenty-five years, the goal of computer developers has been to rid the computer of keyboards, but more development in the field of character recognition is needed. One way to eliminate the keyboard is to teach computers to read through optical character recognition. Another way is to recognize the human voice instead of typed data. But speech recognition is not advancing as rapidly as some computer developers would like. It is not likely that the near future will see computers we can converse with because we have no appropriate technology that is this advanced. More promising is the ability of the computer to scan images. Already character recognition machines scan pages of printed material. Computer developers are also considering electronic gloves that could be used by people to point to areas of the screen. There is no limit to what will be coming next in computer development. The result of doing away with the keyboard will be to save time and to eliminate all those typos.

Chapter 15
Transitions

Responses will vary, but one possible revision is provided here.

My father really needs help because he is a workaholic. He works nearly twelve hours a day. Doctors have told him it is not only bad for his health, but it is affecting his family, and he has worried my family to no end. My family has tried to help him, but he has not acknowledged the problem. He has a tolerance that goes through the roof. He sneaks out of the house before anyone is awake, and he gets home after most of us have finished dinner and are getting ready for bed. He works at home as well: his computer is connected to the one at his office, and his work calls him at home. He has a pager and a cell phone. Things may be getting worse since Dad accepted a promotion to regional director.

Chapter 16
Sentence Variety

Responses will vary, but one possible revision is provided here.

Animal rights activists, who are known primarily for their campaigns against fur coats and the use of animals in laboratories, are also campaigning against rodeos. In their public statements seeking support, protesters say that rodeo animals are being mistreated. For example, they say the animals are starving and live a life filled with pain and suffering. Although animal rights activists also say that rodeo horses buck because they are in pain, rodeo and circus owners say that this is not so. Well fed and comfortable, these animals would be going to slaughter if they were not used as show animals. Moreover, to emphasize their point, handlers explain that they have a healthy respect for the size and power of these animals. Treated like star athletes, the animals enjoy performing. On the other hand, animal rights activists point to the use of cattle prods and bucking straps to get the animals moving, but rodeo owners argue that even ranchers have to use electric prods to get herds moving. Before prods were used, ranchers used pitchforks. Calf roping, also condemned by animal rights activists, can break calves' necks and can also snap vertebrae and legs. Calf roping, to the satisfaction of animal rights activists, has been banned in some states. Eliminating calf roping, they hope, can result in the overall elimination of rodeo shows. However, rodeo owners protest that breaking of calves' necks, bones, and vertebrae just doesn't happen, and they invite activists to come to rodeos and see for themselves.

Part Three
Chapter 17
Verbs

17a. Verb Phrases

Some scientists <u>are saying</u> that a buildup of carbon dioxide and other greenhouse gases in the atmosphere <u>will</u> <u>cause</u> global warming. But another group of scientists <u>argue</u> that we <u>should study</u> the data more carefully before any firm conclusions <u>are drawn</u>. While scientists generally <u>agree</u> that an unchecked accumulation of greenhouse gases <u>will</u> <u>cause</u> changes, no one <u>knows</u> when it <u>will start</u>, how much <u>will happen</u>, or how rapidly it <u>will occur</u>. The most widely accepted estimate is that there <u>will be</u> a rise in the earth's average temperature as early as 2050. This <u>could bring</u> rising sea levels and severe droughts In some areas. But <u>no</u> one <u>knows</u> yet how clouds and the ocean's ability to absorb heat <u>will affect</u> this. When scientists <u>understand</u> this better, projections <u>can be revised</u>.

17b. Verb Forms

The evidence that global <u>warming</u> has <u>started</u> is not very strong. Some scientists believe that the concentration of carbon dioxide has <u>increased</u> over 25 percent since the early 1800s, but other scientists point to the fact that the average global temperature has <u>risen</u> by no more than a half degree Centigrade. Even that rise is questionable since there was a <u>cooling</u> period from 1940 to 1970 that caused forecasters <u>to predict</u> a return to the ice ages. Therefore, <u>to</u> <u>act</u> on predictions by <u>passing</u> laws that restrict or ban the use of fossil fuels may be hasty, but <u>conserving</u> energy, <u>banning</u> harmful chlorofluorocarbons, and <u>planting</u> more trees <u>to absorb</u> carbon dioxide from the air seems sensible. Many industries are also <u>acting</u> more responsibly and are <u>reducing</u> hazardous emissions from their factories.

17c. Verb Tense

In 1987, the FBI (<u>opened</u>, has opened, was opening) a $1.5 million mock-up of a small town in Virginia named Hogan's Alley. Presently, the town's population (has been, will be, <u>is</u>) about 200. Generally, Hogan's Alley (has looked, <u>looks</u>, is looking) like any peaceful little American town, but often the quiet (will be shattered, <u>is shattered</u>, had been shattered) by the sound of a shotgun or squealing tires. Then prospective G-men who (had been sitting, sat, will sit) outside the post office jump in their cars and race after the "criminals." None of this (will be, is, is being) real because Hogan's Alley (is, has been, had been) a training academy for those who (will want, want, will have wanted) to become FBI agents. Next year over 500 trainees (will have attended, attend, will attend) classes in frisking, lectures on handcuffing, and seminars on interrogating witnesses. The FBI (started, was starting, had started) Hogan's Alley because it wanted its agents to have more true-to-life experience before they go out and deal with dangerous criminals. So now every day there (will be, have been, are) mock bank robberies, kidnappings, and drug busts. The "criminals," however, are actors, part-time students, retirees, off-duty policemen and firemen, and anyone else who (has passed, will pass, had passed) the rigorous screening tests.

Last year, in Hogan's Alley, the FBI's mock-up village for prospective FBI agents, the trainees took part in an intensive 14-week training course. About 46 agents moved through the program which began with lessons in surveillance. Trainees tracked a suspect from his home as he drove to a shopping mall and sold a small bag of phony cocaine. Next came a class in simple arrests, when agents-in-training burst into a fleabag motel and took an unarmed burglar as he lay in bed. Agents learned how to frisk suspects, and then they read them their rights. Instructors, who brought their own experience as former FBI agents to the teaching, carefully gave advice to each trainee and provided pointers on how to handle details such as slipping on handcuffs during a struggle. Nine weeks into the course, trainees got some practice in arresting an armed felon. Their final lessons took place in a courtroom, where they faced a team of actors who posed as a tough team of defense lawyers. Those trainees who did not flunk out of the course became FBI agents, and the actors, who played drug peddlers, burglars, and other felons, said that seeing what it is like being on the wrong end of the law reminded them that they did not want to become criminals themselves.

17d. Verb Voice

Like many cities built on a river, Kansas City is divided (passive) between two states. The biggest single municipality is Kansas City, Missouri, but over one-half of the population of the metropolitan area lives (active) in various suburban cities on the Kansas side. Problems are created (passive) when it comes time to finance projects that will benefit (active) both sides of the state line. In the 1990s, cities on both sides of the state line agreed (active) to a bi-state sales tax to be used to renovate Kansas City, Missouri's Union Station. Advocates said (active) the new station would bring (active) in tourism that would benefit both sides of the state line. Opponents claimed (active) Kansas City, Missouri was just trying to dip (active) into the pockets of the more affluent suburbs on the Kansas side. In the end, a compromise was reached (passive). The bi-state sales tax was passed (passive), but all contributing cities had (active) a say in its use and the tax had (active) a 5-year duration. It was not renewed (passive).

17e. Verb Mood

Singles bars and dating services are thriving (declarative), but there are always new approaches. In commercial dating services, one new approach that may be cheaper (subjunctive) than the standard videotaped interviews is the lunch-date service. For less than $50 a month, the company promises (declarative) three lunch dates a month. People are paired on the basis of simple criteria gathered from brief interviews that might last (subjunctive) less than five minutes. The company sets up the lunch date, and the participants take it from there. "Meet (imperative) new people," says the advertising brochure, "and enjoy (imperative) some interesting little restaurants." Since the Census Bureau puts (declarative) the number of single adults at 66 million and growing, these new twists on dating services may prosper (subjunctive).

17f. Modal Verbs

When American products began appearing in Moscow, city officials worried that the signs and advertising for these products might make (could possibly make) Moscow look less Russian. A law recently passed in Moscow warns that all stores and businesses must display (need to display) signs in Russian or at least change them into the Cyrillic alphabet. This has caused many businesses to contact the city inspector because of questions they have. For example, one businessman wondered whether he should change (is obliged to change) the letters in the label for the Puma running shoes that he sells. He was concerned that changing the letters from English to Russian might make (has the possibility of making) the shoes less well-known. The problem became confusing because the new law does not forbid foreign words but does require the Russian sign to be bigger than the one in English. Different stores found different solutions. An American cosmetics company, Esteé Lauder, announced that they <u>will</u> put (<u>strongly intend to put</u>) one sign with the Russian alphabet on their awning and another sign with the English alphabet in the windows. Despite all the questions and worries, the inspector in charge of enforcing this rule will be very strict about checking on foreign signs.

Chapter 18
Nouns and Pronouns

18a. Nouns

Sports fanatics are spending large sums of money these <u>days</u> to purchase sports memorabilia. In fact, says one of the <u>industry's spokespersons</u>, it is a $100 million-a-year obsession. Buyers look for scorecards, stadium seats, autographed baseball bats, and even <u>children's</u> clothing that belonged to old-time greats such as Babe Ruth. <u>Ruth's</u> personal letter to a fan recently sold for over $7000. Since Joe Lewis, the famous boxer, kept many of his old <u>mouthpieces</u>, <u>collectors</u> are paying over $2000 for boxed sets of Lewis's mouthpieces. There is even a magazine entitled *Sports Collectors Digest* which keeps <u>collectors</u> informed about many of the <u>auctions</u> and the availability of various <u>items</u> of interest. A faculty member in the history department of a major American university has begun a study of this phenomenon and reports that yearly increases in prices are staggering. For example, he says, a nineteenth-century baseball card of an obscure Hall of Fame pitcher, Tim O'Keefe, which was worth about $750 two <u>years</u> ago, recently sold for over $30,000. <u>O'Keefe's</u> other memorabilia are expected to soar in value as well. Sports <u>collectibles</u> are now big business.

18b. Pronouns

The business of sports collectibles has become so profitable that <u>it</u> has attracted con artists <u>who</u> manage to forge and sell bogus items. The forgeries have become such big business, in fact, that many con artists help <u>one another</u> and have developed a large network of bogus items. <u>These</u> items include fake Joe DiMaggio signatures and imitation press box pins. <u>Anyone who</u> is in the memorabilia business can spot <u>these</u> forgeries and fakes, but sports fans are often too enthusiastic about a purchase to take the time to have <u>their</u> purchases checked by experts. As a result, <u>they</u> often allow themselves to be conned. A lot of junk from people's attics is also cluttering the market. When someone finds yellowed pages from 1929 sports sections in her scrapbook, she may think she has an expensive treasure. Flea markets overflow with these antiques which may or may not be worth anything. But if a buyer is willing to pay large sums of money, who can say whether that autographed photo or threadbare jersey is or is not a treasure worth collecting? With a market where buyers pay $20,000 for one of Lou Gehrig's old bats, it is worth cleaning out those old attics and scrapbooks.

Chapter 19
Pronoun Case and Reference

19a. Pronoun Case

When historian Page Smith began to ask himself just what kind of education was being provided by American universities, he started with a list of questions. His answers can be found in his book entitled *Killing the Spirit*. Those readers looking for encouraging conclusions will not find them in this report as Smith criticizes professors' lack of interest in teaching and their tendency to spend too much time writing books and articles that do not contribute anything useful to mankind's betterment. Smith finds those academics who look down on teaching as less important than research to be at fault. For him, the student revolt of the 1960s and early 1970s was a time when students were looking for answers to important questions but got no help from their professors. There was no dialogue between their professors and them that addressed questions about meaning and values in life, says Smith. However, community colleges and small, independent colleges still concern themselves with the needs of students. University administrators who are more interested in budgets and specific agendas will not find answers in Smith's book, and readers will wonder who his real audience is. To whom should we look for answers?

19b. Pronoun Reference

When Benjamin Franklin discovered electricity in thunderclouds, he sparked a controversy that still has no clear answer. How do clouds become electrified in the first place? To this day they haven't been able to adequately explain how it contains such incredible amounts of electricity that a stroke of lightning can contain about 100 million volts.

One researcher who wants to find some answers flies his plane into storms to measure electric fields and ice particle changes. It's bumpy work, he says, especially if there are large hailstones because <u>it</u> can damage the plane and the measuring equipment. On one trip <u>they</u> noticed that in sections of clouds where water and ice mix, the measuring devices picked up indications of strong charge separation. The answer may be that in a certain temperature range, the temperature can cause the charge separation. Another factor may be a kind of soft hail called "graupel," pea-sized particles that can look like miniature raspberries. <u>They</u> form when droplets of supercooled water collide, freezing together instantly. Ice crystals then bounce off the growing graupel, building up a charge from the friction just as you build up a static electricity charge when you scuff your feet across the carpet. When <u>they</u> are carried to different parts of the cloud, the result is a separation of the positively and negatively charged particles. Then, when the electrical difference between the ground and the sky becomes great enough, everyone should haul his or her kite in.

Chapter 20
Adjective and Adverbs

20a. Adjectives and Adverbs

For <u>many</u> people, <u>the crossword</u> puzzle in <u>the daily</u> paper is one of life's <u>little</u> pleasures. Some say it is <u>also surely</u> one of life's frustrations. While <u>puzzle</u> books <u>conveniently</u> include <u>the</u> answers in <u>the</u> back, <u>most</u> newspapers print <u>the</u> answers <u>the next</u> day. <u>Now</u> there is <u>a quicker</u> answer. <u>Some</u> companies have <u>an automated</u> solution. Readers can dial <u>an 800</u> service for <u>instant</u> answers. <u>This</u> service is <u>free</u> to callers but is paid for by advertisers who sponsor <u>each</u> day's puzzle. <u>An</u> advertiser can run <u>a small</u> advertisement by <u>the</u> puzzle and can include <u>a ten-second</u> message that callers will hear before <u>the</u> answers are given. *The New York Times* handles this <u>differently</u>. For their puzzles, callers pay for <u>all</u> requests for clues. <u>These</u> services are <u>a major</u> breakthrough for <u>frustrated</u> puzzle-doers who are used to waiting until <u>the next</u> day.

20b. A, An, The

After winding down twenty miles of dirt road in Mtunthama, Malawi, (<u>no article</u>) visitors will come upon the well-kept lawns and gardens of (<u>the</u>) Kamuzu Academy, one of (<u>no article</u>) Africa's most unusual schools. Here, on four hundred acres of well-trimmed lands is (a) school dedicated to classical scholarship. (The) school was founded by President Hastings Kamuzu Banda, the ruler of Malawi since it won its independence from (the) British in 1964. Originally, Dr. Banda studied at (a) Scottish missionary school in Malawi and went on to study in (no article) South Africa, (the) United States of America, and (no article) Britain, where he acquired (a) medical degree and (a) love of Latin and Greek, as well as a strong attraction to the classical emphasis of the elite British schools. When Dr. Banda returned to Malawi, he wanted to copy (the) architecture and curriculum of Eton and other British boarding schools. Some critics in opposition to Dr. Banda say that (the) academy is not appropriate in their country where ordinary schools often do not have (no article) textbooks and where more than two-thirds of (the) population are illiterate. However, defenders of the school point out that the school is not elite in choosing its students. Children are accepted without regard to their family's wealth or position. Each year 35,000 students take (an) exam to try to gain entrance to the school which accepts about eighty new students (a) year. Once accepted, all students are required to take four years of (no article) Latin and four years of (no article) ancient Greek, along with (no article) English, (no article) mathematics, and (a) history course about Africa. Most graduates go on to university and then take jobs in (the) Malawi civil service.

20c. Comparisons

1. larger
2. largest
3. more exciting
4. most enjoyable
5. user-friendliest (or most user-friendly)
6. better
7. best
8. worst

Chapter 21
Prepositions

Americans used to pour ketchup over so many foods that it was America's favorite condiment. Now salsa has replaced ketchup as the favorite <u>between</u> the two <u>in</u> American food markets. Salsa, which means "sauce" <u>in</u> Spanish, is defined as any fresh-tasting, chunky mixture, usually made with tomatoes, chilies, onions, and other seasonings. Although salsa used to be associated <u>with</u> Mexican and southwestern cooking, it is being used for a variety of foods not particularly Mexican. The popularity <u>of</u> salsa is apparently part of the current food trend as Americans become more interested <u>in</u> spicier foods. In 1988, only 16 percent of households <u>in</u> America bought salsa. <u>In</u> two years, that figure was up to 36 percent, and the market continues to grow <u>at</u> a very fast rate. A marketing information company notes that salsas and picantes—which are different <u>from</u> salsas because they are thinner—account <u>for</u> about two-thirds of this market, a category that also includes taco and enchilada sauces. As the market expands, so do the choices. The simplest salsas are based <u>on</u> chopped tomatoes and chilies, and the types of chilies determine how hot the particular type of salsa is. Cookbooks with a variety of recipes indicate the preference of some people to make their salsas <u>at</u> home. Salsas are one of the few popular snack foods that are fat-free or nearly so, and many are made without preservatives, two characteristics that may contribute <u>to</u> their popularity now that people are interested <u>in</u> eating healthier. Riding on this wave of popularity are the new fruit salsas, made with peaches, pineapples, and so on, and vegetable salsas, made with pinto beans, corn, and black-eyed peas. Other varieties will surely appear as the market expands <u>in</u> the future.

Chapter 22
Subjects

Because television <u>viewers</u> of sporting events like to follow the actions of specific players, a cable <u>company</u> in New York is trying out a new subscription service. If <u>it</u> is successful, <u>it</u> is likely to become available to everyone. Cable <u>subscribers</u> will be able to tune into a tournament and pick the player <u>they</u> want to follow. Using a wand similar to a TV remote control, <u>viewers</u> sitting at home will be able to switch from conventional network coverage to a <u>camera</u> that focuses solely on the preferred player. Instant <u>replays</u> and a <u>list</u> of statistics on selected pros will be other selections that the <u>service</u> will provide. This interactive <u>technology</u> will allow viewers to customize programming. While the present <u>programming</u> is only a test of the technology, some cable <u>companies</u> foresee customers being able to sign up for interactive television just like other cable services. When will this service be available for everyone? It is too soon to know for sure, but there is certainly a large demand for such services.

Chapter 23
Phrases

1. c

2. b

3. f

4. c

5. e

6. a

7. d

Chapter 24
Clauses

24a. Independent Clauses

If you are a magician and like highly structured organizations, you may want to join either the International Brotherhood of Magicians or the Society of American Magicians. If, however, you are a magician who lives in New York City and likes to gather informally with other magicians, you should visit Reuben's Restaurant on 38th Street and Madison Avenue any Saturday afternoon. There will be professional and amateur magicians sitting in the back room, and they will be swapping tricks or polishing their routines on each other. People come in with jumbo interlocking rings, decks of cards, and brightly colored scarves in their pockets. Some are doctors, professors, salespersons in shoe stores, tax attorneys, shipping clerks, or teenagers who are just learning the basics. Others are professionals who have appeared on *The Tonight Show* or in traveling circuses. They all share a love of magic, and they willingly sit and watch each other's routines because they know how valuable it is to keep practicing.

24b. Dependent Clauses

There are an estimated 50,000 magicians in America. Most are amateurs <u>who enjoy magic as a hobby</u>. These amateurs often have elaborate equipment <u>although their only audience is usually their friends and relatives</u>. Some, however, specialize in the small card, coin, and rope tricks <u>that are always popular</u>. Purists call this intimate "close-up" magic the only real magic <u>because it relies so heavily on a person's manual dexterity</u>. <u>Because people seem to prefer to be fooled face-to-face</u>, this close-up magic is also offered by professional magicians <u>who perform at birthday parties and trade shows</u>. A psychologist <u>who is also a magician</u> says <u>that when something is done under people's noses</u>, it's more magical. It's much more elusive. The spectacular effects of magic done on television don't seem to impress people quite so much. <u>Whatever the cause may be</u>, amateur magicians will keep buying those sponge balls, decks of cards, special coins, and paper flowers.

Chapter 25
Essential and Nonessential Clauses and Phrases

Responses will vary, but one possible revision is provided here.

Music teachers in the elementary schools <u>who want to teach classical music to their students</u> now have a lot of materials to help them. The materials have been developed by a group of educators who <u>want to introduce classical music appreciation programs in elementary schools</u>. Many students say these materials are excellent. These programs are also being used to coach students for contests. The programs incorporate listening skills and information about themes, styles, and forms of music. Students seem to enjoy these contests. The contests are a new form of competition in many schools. Contestants are often asked to identify the main themes of familiar works such as *Nutcracker Suite*, the specific instruments being played, and the composers. Harder questions are those that are asked about music the students have not studied in school. These questions stump even the more experienced teams. Not all the music <u>that is studied in the music appreciation classes</u> is classical. Sometimes jazz and non-Western music is added, though students also seem to enjoy studying classical music <u>that they have heard on television commercials</u>. Music teachers <u>who have tried these programs</u> are pleased with the variety of types of music students come to like and the quantity of music they come to know. These music appreciation programs are expanding rapidly across the nation. The programs were begun on a small scale in a few states.

Chapter 26
Sentences

1. c

2. c

3. e

4. b

5. e

6. c

7. a

8. a

9. e

10. d

11. c

Part Four

Chapter 27
Commas

27a. Commas in Compound Sentences

In 1977 the flight of the little airplane, the Gossamer Condor, did not look very impressive, but it was indeed a historic flight. With wings of foam, balsa wood, and Mylar, the plane designed by Paul MacCready floated slowly and gracefully over the San Joaquin Valley and covered a mile or so in about eight minutes. What made it so historic was that the pilot was pedaling. The Gossamer Condor was only the first of MacCready's pedal-powered planes, and two years later the plane's successor, the Gossamer Albatross, crossed the English Channel. Some people say that MacCready is really the brains behind these inventions, but others feel that he receives undue credit for the work that others on the development teams do. However, MacCready was the first to use his observations of how birds fly, so his supporters feel that he is the genius who made human-powered flight possible. Other inventors were taking the conventional approach of trying to reduce drag as much as possible because they thought this approach would be the answer. The approaches of other inventors were to streamline their aircraft, or they tried to incorporate ways to increase the horsepower. Only MacCready applied the principle of vastly increasing the wing area and used materials to keep the overall weight down. The result was an aircraft that needed only the power output of a good bicyclist, and the Gossamer Condor now has a place of honor next to the *Spirit of St. Louis* in the Smithsonian Institute's National Air and Space Museum.

27b. Commas After Introductory Words, Phrases, and Clauses

Having won prizes with his first human-powered plane, Paul MacCready went on to build a faster and more powerful pedal-powered plane, the Gossamer Albatross. In less than two years after his first success, MacCready's second pedal-powered plane departed from Folkestone, England, in June, 1979, bound for France. Expecting the flight to take about two hours, MacCready allotted just enough water for the pilot to drink. The flight team who prepared the plane and assisted the pilot on the ground waited several weeks for the kind of calm weather that was needed. Consequently, the pilot took off, expecting to reach France before his endurance and the water gave out. But a head wind blew up soon after the pilot was aloft. An hour and a half later, he was only two-thirds of the way to France, and his legs were cramping from all the pedaling. Because everyone was sure they had to give up the attempt, the flight team was ready to hook a towline to the craft that would haul it ashore. Tired and about to give up, the pilot knew he had to gain altitude to get hooked to the towline. As he climbed, he found less wind and was able to press on. Almost three hours later, the pilot touched down at Cape Gris-Nez, in France, a minute short of his theoretical exhaustion point. The Gossamer Albatross had crossed the English Channel, powered only by the pilot.

27c. Commas with Essential and Nonessential Words, Phrases, and Clauses

After designing human-powered planes, Paul MacCready, a prize-winning inventor, went on to design a solar-powered plane. MacCready, however, realized that solar cells as an energy source for planes do not make any practical sense. But MacCready, who had long sympathized with environmental concerns, hoped to demonstrate that solar power has an important part in the world's energy future. Those who see solar energy

as merely a minor source of energy for the future downplay the importance of such demonstrations. Others think solar

power has simply not been adequately developed for practical use. The solar-powered plane that MacCready designed

flew from Paris to the coast of England in 1981, cruising at 441 mph at an altitude of 11,000 feet. The plane, called the

Solar Challenger, provided the stepping stone to MacCready's next flying machine, the Sunraycer, a solar-powered

car.

27d–h. Commas in Series and Lists; Commas with Adjectives; Commas with Dates, Addresses, Geographical Names, and Numbers; Other Uses for Commas; Unnecessary Commas

The Sunraycer, which is a solar-powered lightweight car, was built to compete in the 1987 Race Across Australia.

Designed by Paul MacCready, the car won the race from Darwin to Adelaide and is now in the Smithsonian Institute's

National Museum of American History. With a total weight of 365 pounds, the car has a power output of about 1.8

horsepower at noon on a bright day, and it gets the electric power equivalent of 500 miles to the gallon. The

Sunraycer, which presently holds the solar-powered speed record of 48.7 mph, averaged a little over 40 mph for much

of the race. The car is so light that when it made turns during testing, it often seemed in danger of blowing over. The

engineers who worked on the Sunraycer ended up putting two little ears on the top. "We're not sure why they work,"

said one engineer, "though they seem to help." In some ways the Sunraycer is not a prototype of electric cars for

commercial use because the Sunraycer has bicycle-thin wheels, a driver's seat that requires the driver to lay flat, and

very weak acceleration. However, many of Sunraycer's features were carried over into the electric car developed by

General Motors. Like the Sunraycer, the GM car uses alternating current and can, therefore, get better performance. If

electric-powered cars become widely popular in the future, Paul MacCready will feel that he had some small part in

saving the environment.

Chapter 28
Apostrophes

In the game of baseball, batting slumps are one of a player's worst nightmares. When they are doing well, players attribute their successes to mysterious minor occurrences around them that then become habits_ the players keep up. After a game in which one baseball player who was wearing an old helmet with it_s side dented hit two triple_s, a home run, and a single, the player continued to wear that helmet for the rest of the season. Warding off evil spirits through superstitions is another thing baseball players do. One player always wears the green T-shirt from his_ university under his team's jersey. Another won't wear a jersey with any 6's in his player's number. Batting coaches spend hours watching videotapes with slumping players, trying to find what's causing the problem. They examine the player's batting stance or swing, but this does_n't always provide useful clues. Some slumps happen when batters begin to worry too much about their misses and about everyone else's successes. But one coach thinks otherwise. He notes that some players_ start making adjustments when they've hit a double and want to hit farther or when a certain unusual pitch connected well with their bats. Players in their 30's_ complain of a different kind of slump. One bad day, says one over-30 player, may mean he is losing it, that his age has begun to take it_s toll. A hitter who is hot, on the other hand, tends to get possessive about a special bat and uses it until it breaks or its_ cracks begin to show. When that bat goes, the player sometimes loses confidence until he connects with a new bat that brings him a few homeruns_. A batter_s life is_n't as easy as some people think it is.

Chapter 29
Semicolons

Junk mail used to be confined to print on paper; now it is appearing in people's mailboxes on videocassettes. Companies in the direct-mail business are now marketing inexpensive cardboard videocassettes that can carry a variety of messages, such as audiovisual advertisements, promotional premiums, and educational or training aids. Some companies are switching to this form of direct-mail advertising because it is relatively cheap; in addition, it presents messages more vividly on television screens than print advertising can on paper. Informational videos can be sent to prospective customers, and advertisers can use their product in the video. Says the spokesperson for one cereal company, "We are interested in promoting good nutritional habits"; as might be expected, the balanced diet they will be picturing in the video will include their cereal. Printed instructions in merchandise are often confusing;

consequently, some manufacturers are also switching to these disposable videocassettes for the instructional packets they include with their merchandise. The cardboard videocassettes are relatively cheap to manufacture and cheap to mail. They are certainly more convenient than the promotional packets sent by companies that have relied on enclosing sample packets of toothpaste, aspirin, or cereal; mail advertisers who send bulky envelopes of coupons; and companies who want to entice customers with big brochures of vacation places, hotels, and tours. The disposable videocassette is certainly going to grow in popularity as an advertising medium.

Chapter 30
Colons

Evaluating college teachers is a complex, often difficult task. Now a new method devised in the Midwest is being tried out across the nation: the teaching portfolio. Administrators and faculty members see the portfolio, a collection of materials documenting classroom performance, as a way to emphasize teaching as a major priority. Too often, professors who are being evaluated document primarily their research and scholarly activities, such as published books and articles, lists of grants, and conference presentations. Says one faculty member at a large Eastern university: "When it comes to teaching, most teachers only have student evaluations and coffee-room conversations about what they do in class and how their students are learning"; this kind of evidence is not very thorough or sufficient to determine pay raises, tenure, and promotion. As a result, many faculty members are judged and rewarded on the basis of their research and publications. Their teaching performance, whether outstanding or mediocre, is largely ignored. The portfolio can be a better measure of what faculty really do as teachers, for the portfolio can consist of the following items: a statement of the person's teaching philosophy, a list of the courses that person has taught, a representative syllabus, statements by fellow faculty members who have observed this person, and course materials that the person has prepared. At some schools where portfolios are already in use, the portfolios also include unsolicited letters from former students, teaching awards, and even videotapes of the candidate teaching a class. Some faculty members who have prepared these portfolios say that there is an added advantage: the portfolio collection can lead to self-improvement. This can happen when the process of creating the collection causes the person to think seriously about teaching goals, strategies, and results.

Chapter 31
Quotation Marks

"Why am I fatter than my sister-in-law? I eat less," complained a woman being studied by a team of researchers. She explained that she repeatedly went on diets when her sister-in-law didn't. But the woman continues to weigh more. Researchers are finding out that heredity, in addition to lifestyle, exerts a strong influence on people's weight. By studying identical and fraternal twins, research teams are finding that brothers and sisters end up with similar body weights whether or not they are raised in different families. In the "Journal of Genetics," Dr. Albert Skinnerd writes, "When the biological parents are fat, there is an 80 percent chance that their children will also be overweight" (234). "Does this mean that my brother and I are doomed to be fat?" asked one overweight twin in the study. Since some sets of twins tend to transform extra calories into fat while other sets of twins tend to convert extra calories into muscle, one scientist concluded that "genes do seem to have something to do with the amount you gain when you overeat." Some unsuccessful dieters may be relieved to know that their failed diets aren't a matter of failed willpower. "It is really a matter of metabolism," reports another doctor doing research in this field. But that does not mean that low-fat diets and exercise should be given up. " 'Quit' is not a word in my vocabulary," says one constant dieter who manages to maintain a reasonable weight by means of careful eating and plenty of exercise, despite a tendency to be overweight.

Chapters 32, 33, 34
Hyphens, End Punctuation, and Other Punctuation

Which oils are good for us to eat? A study of thirty-nine participants on a reduced-fat diet looked at the benefits of consuming olive oil and/or corn oil. Which is more beneficial in influencing high-density lipoprotein levels—corn oil or olive oil? This is an important question because high-density lipoprotein (HDL) is considered a beneficial form of cholesterol that helps remove the more dangerous low-density lipoproteins from the body. In a study published in an article, "Two Healthy Oils for Human Consumption" (*Diet and Health News* 14 [1991]: 22–36), researchers report that the participants first spent twelve weeks on a diet that included olive oil and then another twelve weeks on a corn-oil diet. The results (which were also announced on television newscasts) indicated that neither diet resulted in lower levels of HDL. This indicates that a diet of olive oil and/or corn oil can accompany a reduced-fat diet. For those who self-select the oils they use in their diet, the choice is probably a matter of taste or cost.

"Do you see that green area to the left of the river we are flying over?" said the pilot to the passengers as the commercial 747 jet flew over southern Texas. Continued the pilot, "That's my grandfather's ranch. I often visited there as a kid." Public address systems in commercial planes are now being used by pilots to enliven their passengers' flights. Some pilots are opposed to this practice because they see it as a distraction. Says one seasoned veteran, "Our task... is to fly the plane, not amuse the passengers." But others disagree. Interesting, informative comments can put nervous passengers more at ease and can shorten a long flight. For those pilots interested in making such public-address announcements, there is now a book put together by an ex-pilot which pinpoints more than 1,200 historical and little-known places of interest on a collection of highway maps of the U.S. The maps are overlaid with the flight paths used by commercial pilots. Are you flying between El Paso, Texas, and Las Vegas, New Mexico? If so, then look for the site of the Berringer Crater, where a meteor hit with such force 22,000 years ago that it killed all animal and plant life within 100 miles! Thousands of these maps have been sold, with more frequent fliers than pilots doing the buying. "We are learning...an awful lot about territory we thought we knew!" says one frequent flier who takes her book with her on every flight. Another customer reports, "I bought one for my uncle who hates airplanes, and he now actually enjoys his flights." The book is obviously a success. Is the author correct when he says, "Soon, there will be such books in the pocket of every seat in every commercial flight"?

Part Five

Chapters 35, 36, 37
Capitals, Abbreviations, and Numbers

One of Boston's most popular folk heroes is Paul Revere, whose midnight ride was made famous in Longfellow's poem, "Paul Revere's Ride," in Tales of a Wayside Inn. Not many tourists realize that many of the places mentioned in that poem are still part of Boston's twentieth-century landscape, along what is commonly called the Freedom Trail. This well-marked trail is actually a two-mile line in red paint, bricks, or steps with twenty-one historic buildings, sites, and monuments documenting Boston's contribution to American history. Two miles isn't long, but it usually takes tourists who are thorough two or three days to see everything on the trail. Most begin at the Boston Common, the oldest public park in the <u>United States</u>. Here colonists used the public land for grazing animals, training the militia, and staging public executions. Immediately next to the Common is America's first public botanical garden, the Boston Public <u>G</u>arden, famous partly because it was the setting for the well-known children's book, *Make Way for Ducklings*. Just across the <u>s</u>treet, on Beacon Street, is another of Boston's famous sites, the Old State House, completed in <u>1798</u>. Its cornerstone was laid by Samuel Adams in 1793. <u>One</u> block <u>e</u>ast on Beacon <u>S</u>treet and then <u>one</u> block south on Park <u>S</u>treet is the historic Park <u>S</u>treet Church on the corner of Tremont. Here the song "America" was first sung on July 4, 1831. The next stop on the Freedom Trail is the Granary <u>B</u>urying Ground, a <u>c</u>emetery on Tremont Street. Some of the greatest U.S. patriots, including Paul Revere, Samuel Adams, John Hancock, James Otis, etc<u>.</u>, are buried here. Also along Tremont <u>S</u>treet, at the corner of School <u>S</u>treet, is King's Chapel, the first <u>A</u>nglican church in Boston. After the revolution, it became the first <u>U</u>nitarian church in the country, and its cemetery contains the graves of many other early notables, including William Dawes, Jr<u>.</u>, and Gov<u>.</u> John Winthrop. (<u>I</u>t was <u>Governor</u> Winthrop who headed the group that founded the Boston colony.) Also on School Street is the first public school in <u>A</u>merica, which later became the Boston <u>P</u>ublic <u>L</u>atin School. Rev<u>.</u> Cotton Mather, Ralph Waldo Emerson, John Hancock, Benjamin Franklin, et al<u>.</u>, were alumni of this <u>s</u>chool. These are only a few of the many sights along the Freedom Trail. Longfellow's poem says, "<u>H</u>ardly a man is now alive who remembers that famous night and ride...." True, but the Freedom Trail helps visitors realize many of the events that led to our <u>n</u>ation's independence.

Chapter 38
Underlining/Italics

1. U

2. U

3. Q

4. U

5. U

6. Q

7. Q

8. U

9. U

10. Q

11. U

12. Q

13. U

14. Q

15. U

16. U

17. U

18. U

19. Q

20. U

Chapter 39
Spelling

39a. Proofreading

Inventors of gadgets for automobiles <u>haven't</u> always been successful with <u>their</u> inventions. But we can see from some <u>of</u> these inventions that people have been looking for ways to make cars more <u>functional</u>, better looking, and more fun to drive. <u>For</u> example, we now have <u>elegant</u> and sophisticated ways to <u>hear</u> music in <u>our</u> cars, but some of the earlier ways to add music to driving seem a bit odd now. In the <u>1920s</u>, Daniel Young <u>received</u> a patent for an organ he invented for use in automobiles. He built organ keyboards that could be attached to <u>the</u> back of the front seat so that people riding in the back could play the organ to entertain themselves. This may have been a good idea, except for one thing. The roads of that time, unfortunately, were so bumpy and uneven that the sounds produced by the organ when the car was moving were anything but beautiful. Another terrific idea that didn't make it was Leander Pelton's patent for a car that could be parked by standing it on end. Instead of a back bumper, he built a vertical platform with rollers attached. When parking the Vertical-Park Car, the driver needed to tip the car back onto the platform. Then he could just shove the car into any appropriately sized space. To perform this task, however, was a bit difficult as Pelton never quite explained how the car was to be tipped from horizontal to vertical and back down again. A different problem was that Pelton didn't provide any way to keep gasoline, water, and oil from spilling once the car was up on its parking rollers. But the government gave him a patent; he simply couldn't get anyone to manufacture his Vertical-Park Car. Another invention that never made it was designed by Joseph Grant in 1926—an automobile washing machine. The machine didn't wash cars, but it supposedly washed clothes. Grant's invention consisted of a tub and paddles that bolted to the car's running boards. When the tub was filled with water, soap, and dirty clothes, the bouncing of the car over rough roads provided all the power and agitation necessary to clean a load of dirty clothes. For really dirty loads, an extra twenty miles or so of driving was recommended.

39c. Some Spelling Guidelines

39c. (1) IE/EI

1. believe

2. yield

3. seize

4. height

5. foreign

6. weird

7. field

8. eight

9. deceive

10. financier

11. neither

12. ceiling

13. niece

14. neighbor

15. vein

39c. (2) Doubling Consonants

1. napping

2. footing

3. starred

4. tapping

5. writing

6. referred

7. hopped

8. occurrence

9. beginning

10. benefited

11. shopping

12. omitted

39e. Sound-Alike Words (Homonyms)

1. except

2. accept

3. affected

4. effect

5. here

6. It's

7. it's

8. its

9. passed

10. than

11. then

12. then

13. there, their

14. to, too

15. were

16. who's

17. you're, your

18. advice, buying

19. site

20. quite

21. stationary

22. already

23. all right

24. any one

25. all together

Part Six

Chapter 40
Sexist Language

Responses will vary, but one possible revision is provided here.

In many suburban housing developments built during recent decades there are homeowners associations that enforce housing codes on all the homeowners. The average owner in such a suburb may think that they are free to paint their houses whatever color they like or park any kind of car in their driveways, but that is not the case. Homeowners associations often have a lawyer who spends his or her days enforcing the laws enacted by these associations. The laws see to it that all the members abide by the group's standards of good taste. No plastic flamingos are allowed on the lawn, and all house painters who work in the suburb know that they cannot use certain colors for house trim, such as bright pink or a gaudy yellow, because they have to follow community guidelines. When houses are built in new developments, there are usually restrictive covenants that force buyers to join the association, whether they like it or not. Even when people challenge the laws, they usually lose as the covenants are legally binding. It all starts with the builder because when builders build, they want to make certain that the land value for the community stays high so that they can continue to sell their houses at a good price. The builder often starts off as the chairperson of the homeowners association so that he or she can guide the formation of the rules and regulations. In one wealthy Florida community there are even regulations for local government and civil servants, including dress codes for police officers, taxi drivers, and mail carriers. The only challenges that have gotten through the courts are those that show some regulation discriminates on the basis of race, religion, sex, or other characteristics of the homeowner.

Chapter 41
Unnecessary Words

41a. Conciseness

Responses will vary, but one possible revision is provided here.

Telling time is of great importance to us all, even though the concept of time has changed. Time is important in people's lives because it is the essential measure against which other important measurements are made. For example, we measure our bodies' heart rates and how fast our cars travel in terms of time. We organize our days and nights into segments of time, and from the beginnings of civilization people have counted the passage of time by counting sunrises and sunsets or the movements of the moon and the sun. For centuries speculation about the nature of time was mostly a philosophical discussion of how people perceive time and experience its passage. But in twentieth-century science, since Albert Einstein, physicists have come to realize that time is a dimension of the physical universe. Time is a measure of motion in space, not some philosophical or theoretical thing that exists in people's minds. Einstein also showed that time is not absolute or unique. People used to think that any event measured in time would be seen to take the same amount of time. That is, two clocks in accurate working order would agree on the time interval between two events. But the discovery that the speed of light appeared the same to every observer, no matter how he or she was moving, led to the theory of relativity. Now time is seen to be relative to the observer who measures it. Each observer can have his or her measure of time as recorded by the clock he or she carries. Clocks carried by different observers do not necessarily have to agree. This is a very different view of time from the older one that time is absolute. However, even with this notion that time is not absolute, we still use time as a means of measurement.

Chapter 42
Appropriate Words

42c. Levels of Formality

Responses will vary, but one possible revision is provided here.

Parents concerned about their infants being kidnapped have a new method for identifying the baby. In the past, parents have photographed the child or taken a set of fingerprints to store in computer banks. But these methods are not foolproof. Photographs can be deceiving, especially as children grow up, and fingerprints can be difficult to match. Now scientists concerned about the lack of methods to positively identify a baby have found a promising new approach. Couples can take a sample of their child's DNA material, which contains a large amount of genetic information unique to that child. A repository for storing this information has been set up in New Jersey. The files in this storage facility are then available for matching a sample to a strand of hair, a piece of skin, or a few drops of blood. This DNA "fingerprinting" can positively identify a child at any time in his or her life. The samples in storage can last for the individual's lifetime and many years beyond. Some adults, such as those in high-risk or dangerous occupations, have also become interested in being put on file.

42e. General and Specific Words

Responses will vary, but one possible revision is provided here.

People like driving up for fast food, and now so do their <u>spaniels and collies</u>. A new fast-food industry has begun for drive-in dog food, and the menu is entirely for <u>dogs</u>. These new <u>businesses</u> offer treats to dogs with dog biscuits shaped to resemble <u>the kind of fast food people have</u>. The dog biscuits are made from <u>foods</u> that help keep dogs healthy. The biscuits are <u>flavored differently</u> so that dogs don't get tired of the same thing. Customers love the idea of going to a doggy drive-in after picking up their own <u>fast food</u>. So far the menu has been limited to dog biscuits, but <u>some people</u> will come up with new ideas for better <u>food products</u> for dogs.

42f. Concrete and Abstract Words

Responses will vary, but one possible revision is provided here.

When hikers reach a stream, they often decide to cross where the <u>dirt trail slopes down to</u> the water. But this may not be the best place at which to cross. Water usually moves most swiftly at the narrowest part of the stream. So, hikers should instead look for another spot where the stream widens. Here the current often <u>slows down</u> and may be easier to walk through. When hikers are carrying a backpack, they should loosen the shoulder straps and hip belt before <u>wading in</u> so that they can toss off the pack <u>if they stumble or lose their balance</u>. Some hikers find that if they suddenly hit a depression in the streambed, the weight of the backpack can toss them off balance. Another aid to crossing a stream is a good hiking stick. It can serve as another leg, offering better balance when there are <u>slippery rocks underfoot</u>. It is helpful to remove unneeded <u>sweaters, heavy pants, or boots</u> before crossing a stream with a swift current because the water can drag against <u>waterlogged vests and jeans</u>. The hiker should also take each step slowly and deliberately. The forward foot should be planted firmly before the rear foot is moved. Finally, the careful hiker never hurries across a stream.

42g. Denotation and Connotation

Responses will vary, but possible responses are provided here.

1. famous

2. pushy

3. conservative

4. compulsive

5. sanitary engineer

6. used

7. soil

8. smell

9. cheap

10. lavish

Part Seven

Chapter 44
Verbs

When people from other countries <u>will shop</u> in American supermarkets, they find an amazing supply of items

other than grocery items. On one aisle, a shopper <u>will discovered</u>, for example, toiletry items such as toothbrushes,

toothpaste, deodorant, and shampoo. On another aisle <u>be</u> paper towels, garbage bags, and cleaning supplies.

Sometimes the choices <u>would be</u> confusing. But the choices <u>do not ended</u> with the shopping itself. Even when the

shopping <u>have conclude</u>, the shopper may have decisions to make. For example, the person behind the checkout

counter <u>may asked</u> if the customer <u>would want</u> the purchases in a plastic bag. Of course, if Americans <u>was</u> to shop in

stores and bazaars in other countries, they <u>can</u> find the process just as confusing.

In the United States, students hope <u>to learn</u> more than just the subject matter they are studying. They believe that

if they <u>study</u> a subject thoroughly, ask questions, and even <u>disagree</u> with certain opinions of writers and scholars, they

<u>will become</u> better thinkers as well. Students from other countries may find it difficult at first to practice critical-

thinking skills in American classrooms because <u>questioning</u> an authority or the written word may be a sign of disrespect in their country. Another problem that students from other countries may encounter in American classrooms involves writing assignments. Whereas American students are comfortable with <u>choosing</u> topics for writing that argue accepted ideas, students from other countries may have difficulty <u>expressing</u> their opinions without <u>apologizing</u> for them because <u>discussing</u> controversial topics may be considered rude in their country. Obviously, students' cultural backgrounds affect many aspects of college life, including how they approach the educational experience.

Chapter 45
Omitted Words

When importing ivory became illegal in the United States in 1989, engineers and material scientists searched for substitutes for natural ivory. For piano makers, the ban on ivory brought on the problem of how to make piano keys after the supply on hand <u>was</u> used up. While conservationists and elephant lovers want people <u>to</u> stop using ivory, many pianists who have tested plastic substitutes <u>are</u> about to abandon hope of having new pianos with satisfactory substitutes. However, <u>there</u> may be a solution. A team of experts has produced a substitute that may satisfy many piano builders and piano players. This new synthetic ivory both resembles natural ivory and has a similar microscopic structure. But even with a substitute for piano keys now available, the market for ivory <u>may</u> not decrease as piano makers <u>have</u> never been major consumers of ivory. The largest consumers of ivory in the world are Asian manufacturers of signature stamps, but even <u>they</u> have given up their use of ivory and <u>are</u> switching to substitutes.

Chapter 46
Repeated Words

1. Students in my class <u>they</u> are looking forward to the upcoming vacation.

2. The book that I wanted to read <u>it</u> was not in the library.

3. My teacher found the book that I left <u>it</u> in the classroom.

4. The apartment building where I live <u>there</u> has two swimming pools.

5. The child returned the dog that I had lost <u>it</u>.

6. The pie in the refrigerator <u>it</u> is for tonight's party.

7. The book drop where library books are placed <u>there</u> is full.

8. My aunt called on the new cellular telephone that she had <u>it</u> installed in her car.

Chapter 47
Count and Noncount Nouns

In American supermarkets, new <u>products</u> and <u>produce</u> are constantly being added to the shelves. Children are attracted to new snack foods, and adults are frequently tempted to buy items with <u>information</u> about health benefits. To increase consumer <u>confidence</u> in package labeling, the Food and Drug Administration has announced new <u>guidelines</u> for various claims food manufacturers add to their labels. Products that are advertised as "low <u>fat</u>" have to provide <u>evidence</u> on the label and meet new government <u>standards</u>. For items that appeal to children, the amount of <u>sugar</u> must be clearly indicated. Particularly helpful are the new regulations on serving size because consumers in America have become very conscious of the amount of <u>protein</u> and <u>fat</u> that they eat as well as the number of <u>calories</u>.

Chapter 48

Adjectives and Adverbs

48c–d. A/An/The, Some/Any, Much/Many, Little/Few, Less/Fewer, Enough, No

In northern India there is <u>a</u> conflict between wildlife officials and Gujjar herders of water buffalo. <u>The</u> Indian Government wants to turn the area into a national park, to be called the Fajaji National Park, but for the last ten years, local water buffalo herders refuse to move off the land. The Gujjars keep herding their water buffalo, despite warnings that the animals are eating up too <u>much</u> of the vegetation and that soon there will be <u>few</u> areas that have not been destroyed by the herding. Several decades ago, the Gujjars agreed to migrate every summer to give the forests a chance to grow again, but communities in the areas they migrated to refused to accept the Gujjars because they needed <u>the</u> land for their own grazing, and they didn't have <u>enough</u> land to share. As a result, the Gujjars now stay in the forest throughout <u>the</u> year. Government officials keep on warning of <u>the</u> dangers of erosion in the forests where Gujjar herding has stripped the land. While <u>some</u> environmental groups say that these forest dwellers have as much right to the land as the animals, other groups support the government's attempt to move the Gujjars. The continued grazing by water buffalos risks using up the <u>few</u> food sources of elephants and other animals. Government officials plan to make <u>an</u> offer to the Gujjars to move them to settlements on the edge of the forests and to have them feed their animals in stalls. Park officials want to find <u>a</u> solution soon because they say that both the park and the Gujjars will suffer if the present situation continues.

Part Eight

Chapter 52
Searching for Information

1. secondary

2. primary

3. secondary

4. secondary

5. primary

6. secondary

Part Ten

Chapter 62
Documenting in Other Styles

1. C

2. E

3. A

4. B

5. D

Part Eleven

Chapter 63
Document Design

63a. Placement and Order

The restaurant guide lists ethnic restaurants two ways:

1. By ethnicity
   - Chinese restaurants
   - Italian restaurants
   - Mexican restaurants
2. By neighborhood

63c.

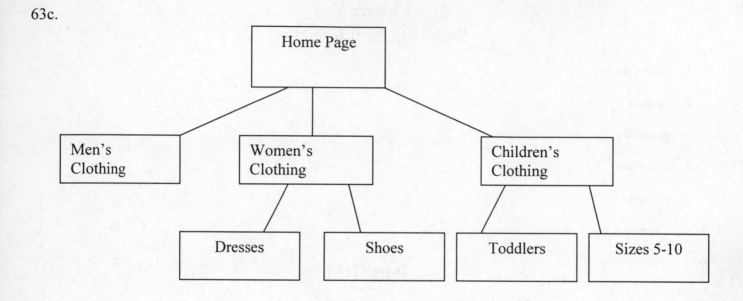

63d. Paper Preparation

1. APA

2. MLA

3. APA

4. APA

5. MLA

6. APA

7. MLA

65d. Conventions in Writing About Literature

1. past tense

2. present tense

3. present tense

4. past tense